The Story of Aston Villa

Aston Villa Football Club

Founded 1874
Colours Claret and blue shirts, white shorts
Ground Villa Park, Trinity Road, Birmingham, B6 6HE
Telephone 021-327-6604
Ground Capacity 48,000
Record Attendance 76,588 v Derby County, FA Cup 6th Rd, 2 March 1946
Record Receipts £167,753 Everton v West Ham (FA Cup Semi-final), 12 April 1980
Pitch measurement 115 yards by 75 yards
Honours First Division Champions 1893-4, 1895-6, 1896-7, 1898-9, 1899-1900, 1909-10. Runners-up 1888-9, 1902-03, 1907-8, 1910-11, 1912-13, 1913-14, 1930-1, 1932-3
Second Division Champions 1937-8, 1959-60; Runners-up 1974-5
Third Division Champions 1971-2
FA Cup Winners 1887, 1895, 1897, 1905, 1913, 1920, 1957; Runners-up 1892, 1924
Football League Cup Winners 1961, 1975, 1977; Runners-up 1963, 1971
Record Win 13–0 v Wednesbury Old Athletic, FA Cup 1st Rd 1886
Record Defeat 1–8 v Blackburn Rovers, FA Cup 3rd Rd 1889
Most League Points gained 70, Third Division, 1971-2
Most League Goals scored 128, First Division, 1930-1
Highest League scorer in a season 'Pongo' Waring, 49, First Division 1930-1
Most League Appearances 560, Charlie Aitken 1961-76
Managers since the War Alex Massie, George Martin, Eric Houghton, Joe Mercer, Dick Taylor, Tommy Cummings, Tommy Docherty, Vic Crowe, Ron Saunders
How to reach Villa Park Bus No 5 from Corporation Street to Whitton Square. Birmingham New Street railway station is near city centre and ground is ½ mile from motorway link.
Address of Supporters Club c/o Villa Park

The Story of
ASTON VILLA

Anton Rippon

Moorland Publishing

British Library Cataloguing in Publication Data

Rippon, Anton
    The story of Aston Villa.
    1. Aston Villa Football Club - History
    I. Title
    796.33'463'0942496   GV943.6.A832

    ISBN 0-903485-99-0

Picture Sources: Illustrations have been provided by: *Birmingham Post & Mail:* 23-6, 32, 43, 45, 47-54, 57-9, 61-2, 64, 67, 69-70, 73, 75-6, 78-9, 81-2, 84-5, 87-8, 90, 92; Colorsport: 6-7, 10 (bottom), 12-14, 16-18, 19 (bottom), 20-2, 27, 29-31, 35-42, 44, 46, 55, 60, 63, 66, 72.
The author and publisher would like to thank Ron Jenkins, Syndications Executive of the *Birmingham Post & Mail,* for help with the provision of illustrations.

ISBN 0903485 99 0

Photoset by Advertiser Printers Ltd, Newton Abbot and printed in Great Britain by Redwood Burn Ltd, Trowbridge & Esher for Moorland Publishing Co Ltd, PO Box 2, 9-11 Station Street, Ashbourne, Derbyshire, DE6 1DZ.

1874-1950

A GOLDEN BEGINNING

According to legend, flickering Victorian gaslights were a favourite spawning ground for football clubs, and the embryo of Aston Villa — one of the greatest names in the history of soccer — was no exception. It was under just such a lamp, in the misty cold of a winter's evening early in 1874 that members of a local Wesleyan chapel lingered on their way home along Heathfield Road, Birchfield, and decided to take up soccer. Over a century later, Heathfield Road has disappeared in a merger with Trinity Road, Aston — which is the postal address of Villa Park. The football team which those young lads founded is now the proud owner of one of the best football grounds in the world; and also of one of the finest pedigrees in the game. The boys already played cricket and although Birmingham was not noted at that time for its soccer, the game held sway in neighbouring towns like West Bromwich and Walsall.

Once the club was formed, it needed a skipper, a ground on which to play, and some opponents. The three requirements posed varying problems. A skipper was soon elected — a young man called W. H. Price — but a ground and opposition were less easily come by. For a start there were very few pure soccer clubs in the city and a game which comprised a curious mixture of association football and rugby was by far the most popular winter game.

It was March 1874 before Aston Villa Football Club could play its first match, and that was against a rugby team! The sides agreed to play forty-five minutes under each code. So Aston Villa began its glorious history by fielding thirteen players against Aston Brook St Mary's on a ground near Birchfield's present-day Wilson Road. The first half was played under rugby rules and Villa managed to reach halftime without any score being recorded for either side. In the second half a round ball was produced and the teams continued the match under soccer rules — or Association (Sheffield) Rules as the code was named. Midway through the second period Villa scored their first-ever goal when Jack Hughes neatly turned the ball past the rugby club's goalkeeper and when the final whistle sounded, they had won their inaugural match 1–0, despite the bizarre nature of its setting.

Villa could not manage another game that season. Of the few other pure soccer teams around, none were considered weak enough to give Aston Villa a fair game. Birmingham Clerks (later Calthorpe FC after their ground at Calthorpe Park) was the top Birmingham club and they, and teams like Wednesbury Old Athletic and Wolverhampton's Stafford Road Works FC, would have demolished that early Villa side. In 1874-5 Villa managed games with such teams as St George's Excelsior and Aston Unity and returned some creditable results, especially considering the youth of their club. Villa's early grounds included Aston Park, close to today's Villa Park, and Aston Lower Grounds Meadow, a venue which had also seen W. G. Grace play against the Australians and a team of American Red Indians introduce the game of lacrosse to Birmingham.

The players who appeared in Aston Villa's first-ever game (a match played against a local rugby team with 45 minutes under each code) were: W. Scattergood, W. Weiss, W. H. Price, F. Knight, E. Lee, G. Matthews, H. Matthews, C. Midgley, J. Hughes, W. Such, H. Whateley, G. Page, A. Robbins, W. B. Mason (secretary), W. Sothers.

Just as we have seen that Victorian gaslamps seemed to play an important part in the early days of English soccer clubs, so too did the arrival of a few Scotsmen. Again, Aston Villa proved no exception to this rule and when a 21-year-old Scot called George Ramsey arrived in Birmingham in 1876, he was set to become one of the prime movers in taking the club on its first steps to greatness. Ramsey was slightly built, but he made up for his lack of physical stature with a display of wizardry which soon had his teammates gasping with admiration. He dribbled round opposing defences wearing a tiny polo cap and soon captured the imagination of the faithful Villa supporters who were now turning up to see the new team play. Villa made him their skipper in 1876 and we shall see how he played an epic part in the club's rise to greatness, both on and off the field.

Yet another Scot was on his way to Birmingham to play a big part in the Villa story. In 1878, Archie Hunter arrived in the city from Ayr to play for the Calthorpe team of which he had heard so much. But fortunately for Villa, Hunter could not find the Calthorpe ground and instead ended up at the Villa ground. He became one of the club's most famous skippers, while Calthorpe Football Club went out of existence as a major force in the game. Meanwhile, the affairs of Aston Villa gathered momentum. Soccer was rapidly gaining a hold in the heavily industrialised Midlands and North and Ramsey began to see that his club needed another ground if they were to take advantage of the ever-growing crowds that were turning up on Villa match days.

It was on a fateful Sunday in 1876 that Ramsey and a fellow Scot called John Lindsay took a stroll to Perry Barr — then a village with a toll gate. Near Wellington Road the far-seeing Ramsey spotted a piece of land used for grazing. Ramsey had found Villa's first real ground. Quickly he discovered that the ground was rented from the Bridge Trust by a local butcher and soon drew up an agreement to sub rent the field from the butcher for £5 per annum. Villa players used a nearby blacksmith's shed for dressing rooms and made their headquarters at The Old Crown and Cushion where Wellington Road met Aston Lane. Villa's first game at Perry Barr was against Wednesbury Town when just twenty-one people paid threepence each to watch the match. Villa's first 'gate' amounted, therefore, to just 5s 3d. But those figures would soon increase many times over as Ramsey and Hunter steered Villa onwards. The team at that time also included such players as Howard Vaughton and Eli Davis who joined Villa from Wednesbury Strollers and played together as the club's left-wing attack. Sam Law played centre-half, and two players wore headgear while they played. Full back Joe Simmonds sported a red cap and Charlie Johnstone appeared in a skull cap.

The Football League was still some years away from its formation (by Villa's William McGregor) but in 1879-80 the club entered the FA Cup for the first time and were drawn away to Stafford Road Works, the powerful Wolverhampton club. Villa made the best possible start to their first-ever Cup campaign. They drew 1-1 at Wolverhampton and won the replay 3-2 to earn a tie with Oxford University. Oxford were then a power in the game and had already played in three FA Cup finals, winning the trophy in 1874. Even so, Villa's attitude to the tie was astounding — they withdrew! To this day, no-one knows why they took this drastic course of action. Whether the prospect of travelling to such a bastion of soccer supremacy daunted them we shall never know. But if it did, it was an act not in keeping with the Villa tradition. At any rate, Oxford went through and finally reached Kennington Oval where they lost the FA Cup final to Clapham Rovers.

Villa did win their first trophy in 1880 when they took the Birmingham Senior Cup and in 1880-1 they again entered the FA Cup, despite their withdrawal of the previous season. In the second round they went to Nottingham and beat Forest 2-1; the draw for the third round sent Villa back to Nottingham, this time to play the 'Notts Club', and they won 3-1. The victory brought Villa face-to-face with Stafford Road Works again and the prospect of a home game against one of the Midlands most powerful sides filled the Perry Barr ground. Alas, Villa fell short of the occasion and the Wolverhampton team won 3-2 to reach the quarter-finals where they were knocked out by the Old Etonians, the eventual losing finalists. Villa's matches in the FA Cup and Birmingham Senior Cup were punctuated with top class friendly matches and on New Year's Day 1881 they had beaten Heart of Midlothian, the famous Edinburgh club, 4-1, Richards, Hunter, Davis and Brown were the Villa scorers.

Aston Villa in 1880. Back row, left to right: J. Hughes, W. McGregor, Mason, Lee, Simmonds, Pank, Davies, F. Johnstone, J. Jeffries. Middle row: Andy Hunter, Ramsay, W. Ellis (President), Archie Hunter, C. Johnstone. Front row, lying: Hall, Ball.

In 1881-2 Villa received a bye into the third round of the FA Cup before beating Forest 4–1 after two drawn games. In the next round, however, Wednesbury Old Athletic beat them 4–2 and their cup involvement was over for another year. But Aston Villa soon came bouncing back and the following season they reached the quarter-finals. Their cup run started with a 4–1 win over Walsall Swifts at Perry Barr. Wednesbury Old Athletic were the next team to fall — by the same score and on the same ground — and then Villa faced Aston Unity in a local derby game. In their third successive home tie Villa won 3–1 and when the draw for the fourth round was made, it pulled Villa out of the hat first yet again, this time against Walsall Town who were beaten 2–1.

In the last eight of the competition for the first time, Villa were forced to travel at last and they found themselves at Trent Bridge, Nottingham, where they faced Notts County. It was an epic cup encounter in the best traditions. County went 3–0 up, for Villa to pull right back into the game at 3–3. Then William Gunn, a famous name in both soccer and cricket, broke away from the Villa defence and scored the winner. But Villa might have forced a replay had the penalty kick been invented at that time. A Notts defender used his hand to divert a shot from goal but the resultant free-kick was not enough to rescue Villa. The club had not much longer to wait, however, before it stamped its name on the coveted FA Cup for the first time. Although they travelled all the way to Glasgow for the 1883-4 fourth round and were soundly beaten 6–1 by Queen's Park, and despite being knocked out in the 1884-5 and 1885-6 early stages, there was glory round the corner.

In 1886-7 Aston Villa became FA Cup holders at last, although it took them ten matches to lift the trophy, including four games with Wolverhampton Wanderers in a marathon tie. Villa had a magnificent

Aston Villa adopted professionalism in 1885 — the same year in which it was legalised in England. Most of the leading clubs in the Midlands and North began to pay their players immediately and Villa could not afford to delay in following suit.

side. George Ramsey had retired to concentrate his efforts on the post of Aston Villa secretary, but there were new faces in a Villa team which lined up in the more familiar positions of two full-backs, three halfbacks and five forwards. Jimmy Warner had taken over in goal from Charlie Hobson and in front of him, Villa had Frank Coulton and Joe Simmonds at full-back in place of Tom Riddell and Alf Jones. On the left-wing Dennis Hodgetts had joined Villa from the local side St George's FC and he lined up on the left flank with Howard Vaughton who, along with Arthur Brown, had been capped by England against the other three Home Countries in the year that Villa had been knocked out of the FA Cup in that thrilling tie at Trent Bridge.

A record number of clubs —132 — entered the FA Cup in 1886-7 and they represented England, Scotland, Ireland and Wales. There were Rangers, Hearts and Partick Thistle from North of the Border; Chirk, amongst several teams from the Principality; and Cliftonville from across the Irish Sea. In the first round Villa started much closer to home, against their old rivals Wednesbury Old Athletic, and won 13–0. Derby Midland were crushed 6–1 in the next stage and Villa moved on to a tie with Wolves. On 11 December 1886 Villa and Wolves drew 2–2 at Perry Barr. Seven weeks later, and after seven and a half hours football, Villa finally won through 2–0, again at

Aston Villa FA Cup winners 1886-7. Back row, left to right: Coulton, Warner, Dawson, Simmonds, Allen. Middle row: Davies, Brown, Hunter, Vaughton, Hodgetts. Front row: Yates, Burton.

Perry Barr, after two matches at Wolverhampton had ended 1–1 and 3–3. The deciding match was played in the teeth of a gale but a record 12,000 braved the conditions to see the marathon finally ended.

Villa were rewarded with a bye in the fourth round — and how they must have needed the rest — before they beat the Lincolnshire side Horncastle 5–0 at Perry Barr. In the quarter-finals, Villa were given a much tougher time by the Lancashire club Darwen, although they led 3–0 at half-time. Darwen almost pulled back into the game and at the end, Villa were more than happy with the 3–2 scoreline.

Glasgow Rangers at Crewe seems an incredible semi-final today; but that is the task which faced Villa in March 1887 and they did well to beat a side comprised solely of Scottish internationals. Aston Villa beat the Scots 3–1 and Birmingham went wild — their team was in the FA Cup final, where they met fellow Black Country club West Bromwich Albion at Kennington Oval. Twenty thousand spectators saw the first-ever all-Midland FA Cup final on Saturday, 2 April 1887. Both sides fielded full-strength teams and in the Albion goal stood their huge goalkeeper Bob Roberts, complete in cricket flannels! Albion won the toss and attacked down the sloping Oval pitch with a strong wind gusting behind them and for the first quarter-of-an-hour, Villa had their defence to thank for being level at 0–0.

It was essential to Villa's hopes that they hung on till half-time and this they did. In the second half, with the advantage of the slope and the fact that Albion had suffered the psychological blow of being unable to capitalise on their first half advantages, Villa took the game and won it convincingly, although their first goal had something of a bizarre nature about it. Roberts made no attempt to save Hodgett's shot, assuming that the winger was off-side. Imagine his horror when referee, Major Marindin, President of the FA, pointed to the centre-circle to signal a goal. Player protests are nothing new, but the major stood his ground as Roberts and the Albion players swarmed round him, and Villa were 1–0 ahead.

Two minutes from the end Villa made it 2–0. Hunter snapped up a badly-judged backpass from an Albion defender and although Roberts came out of his goal to collide with the Villa captain, Hunter was able to poke the ball over the line. When they arrived home at 3am the following morning, Villa were met at the railway station by thousands of fans. Besides the FA Cup, Villa had also won the Birmingham Cup and the Birmingham Charity Cup that season, and on the Saturday after their FA Cup triumph they entertained the Scottish Cup winners Hibernian and beat them 3–0 to end a great season — the first of many. It was to be 1892 before Villa reached the FA Cup final again but in those brief, ensuing years there happened events, not only significant in the affairs of Aston Villa Football Club, but in the history of the game of football itself. By the time they made their second final appearance, Villa were members of the Football League.

> **The Aston Villa team which won the FA Cup for the first time in 1887 was: Warner; Coulton, Simmonds; Burton, Dawson, Yates; Davis, Brown, Hunter, Vaughton, Hodgetts.**

Clubs and their spectators were tiring of the friendly matches which were played when there was no cup football to whet the appetite, like Villa's fifth round tie with Preston in 1887-8 which packed in a record 27,000 to the Perry Barr ground amid scenes of wild confusion, although Villa went down 3–1 and Preston went on to the final. It was a game followed by the formation of the world's first football competition in which each club played every other club home and away. And one of its prime instigators was Villa committeeman William McGregor. McGregor was a draper with premises near Villa Park and he had often spoken of a 'Football League'. After discussing the scheme with Villa's committee, McGregor set off to visit the best clubs in the country. Eventually, enough of the top clubs in the Midlands and North showed interest for McGregor to call a meeting at a hotel in London's Fleet Street. A subsequent meeting was held in Manchester the following month and the Football League was formed (it has never been called the 'English League' because McGregor always hoped that Scottish clubs would join).

> **Aston Villa's first-ever FA Cup meeting with Birmingham City — then Small Heath — was in 1887-8 when Villa won 4–0 at Muntz Street, Small Heath. Green (2), Brown and Allen scored the Villa goals past Small Heath goalkeeper Chris Charsley who later became Chief Constable of Coventry.**

William McGregor, Villa's committeeman — and later ▶
president — who was responsible for the formation of the
Football League in 1888.

When the 1888-9 season kicked off, Villa lined up with eleven other sides and at the end of that first season they had finished runners-up to Preston North End in the following table:-

		P	W	D	L	F	A	Pts
1	Preston	22	18	4	0	74	15	40
2	Aston Villa	22	12	5	5	61	43	29
3	Wolves	22	12	4	6	50	37	28
4	Blackburn	22	10	6	6	66	45	26
5	Bolton	22	10	2	10	63	59	22
6	West Brom	22	10	2	10	40	46	22
7	Accrington	22	6	8	8	48	48	20
8	Everton	22	9	2	11	35	46	20
9	Burnley	22	7	3	12	42	62	17
10	Derby	22	7	2	13	41	60	16
11	Notts County	22	5	2	15	39	73	12
12	Stoke	22	4	4	14	26	51	12

That same season Preston won the FA Cup by beating Wolves 3-0 at Kennington Oval to become the first team to do the double, a feat which Villa would emulate before long, although in 1888-9 they were drubbed 8-1 by Blackburn Rovers in what was, for Villa, a record defeat in the competition. Considering what honours Villa would win in the next few seasons, the 1889-90 campaign was a poor one, as indeed was the following season. First, Villa finished in the bottom four and were only saved from re-election because the League chose to suspend the rules; they were also knocked out of the FA Cup in

the second round by Notts County. Then Villa finished in the bottom four again and this time were obliged to go cap in hand to the League; their FA Cup run ended in the second round again, this time at the hands of Stoke City.

Inspiration was at hand, however, in the shape of another Villa committee stalwart, Frederick Rinder, a Liverpudlian. In 1892, Rinder called a special meeting of Villa members and gained control of the club as financial secretary with a new committee. It was the most fundamental move in the entire history of a club which knows only too well the upheavals of committee and boardroom. Within a decade, Villa had won the League Championship five times, the FA Cup twice and reached another final in Rinder's very first season in charge, when they lost 3-0 to West Bromwich Albion.

As financial secretary, one of Rinder's first jobs was to tighten up security and he had turnstiles installed at Perry Barr. The first time they were used, the gate receipts trebled! There must have been at least one or two Villa gatemen whose standard of living dropped dramatically as a result.

The story of Aston Villa between 1893 and the start of World War I is one of FA Cup wins, League titles, and runners-up spots as the Villa club became the giants of the Edwardian game, starting their epic run when Victoria still reigned and continuing it into the reign of George V. Three men played as big a part as any in this rise to fame. They were John Devey, Charles Athersmith and James Cowan. Devey was a fine inside-forward who joined the Villa club in March 1891 from St George's; he was capped twice by England and only the tremendous form of the Derby County star Steve Bloomer and Preston's John Goodall prevented Devey from adding to those caps.

> **Villa's star forward John Devey actually made his debut for the club as a baseball player. Villa, along with other professional teams, played the American game quite seriously in the nineteenth century. He went on to skipper Villa's soccer team to many honours. He also played cricket for Warwickshire and scored 7,000 runs for them between 1888 and 1907.**

Devey's partner on the right wing was Athersmith, a signing from Unity Gas FC in February 1891. Athersmith was born at Bloxwich but he was soon immersed in the Villa legend and in all he won twelve England caps, playing against all three Home Countries in 1896-7, as well as winning an FA Cup winner's medal and a League Championship medal; it was impossible for a footballer to win more honours at that time. Cowan

John Devey. He made his debut for Villa as a baseball player but was one of English soccer's greatest forwards in the 1890s.

made his name as a great centre-half. He was a Scotsman and although he was a small man his tackling and speed off the mark were better than anything that the football fans of that age had ever seen. He even managed to win the Powderhall Sprint in 1896, obtaining time off for the race, and for training, by complaining to Villa of a back injury. Although he won £80 in prize money, Cowan was later suspended for a month by a Villa committee seething over the way they had been tricked.

Aston Villa in 1891-92. Back row, left to right: Gorman (trainer), H. Devey, Athersmith, Knight, Hunter, Warner, Barton, Brown, G. B. Ramsey (secretary). Front row: Cowan, Dixon, Cox, Hodgetts, Campbell. Harry Devey was the uncle of John Devey.

Villa's epic run began in 1891-2 when they finished fourth in the League and reached the final of the FA Cup. It was the last cup final to be played at the Oval and Villa reached it with some outstanding performances. In the first round they beat the Derbyshire side Heanor Town 4-1 at Berry Barr; in the next they defeated Darwen 2-0 at home; and in the third round they made the short journey to Wolverhampton where Wolves had recently opened their Molineux ground. Over 20,000 spectators saw Villa win 3-1. The semi-final brought them a game with Sunderland at Bramall Lane, Sheffield. Although Sunderland were powering to the League Championship, Villa prevented them from trying for the double by winning 4-1 with Athersmith having a quite superb match. Villa primed themselves for the cup final with a record 12-2 League win over Accrington seven days before the Oval match where they faced West Brom.

> **Aston Villa's team which reached the 1892 FA Cup final — the last to be played at Surrey's Oval cricket ground — was: J. Warner; W. Evans, G. Cox; H. Devey, J. Cowan, J. Baird; C. Athersmith, J. Devey, W. Dickson, D. Hodgetts, L. Campbell.**

Just as Albion's defence had let them down when Villa took the FA Cup from them in 1887, now Villa's rearguard was largely to blame for their defeat in 1892. Geddes headed home Bassett's centre to put Albion a goal ahead, and then Bassett broke away again, and this time it was Nicholl who met his cross to sink their Black Country cousins. Warner was hopelessly out of position when Reynolds scored a third from some forty yards out and on the day, Villa were beaten 3-0 by a much better side. There was more gloom for Warner when irate Villa fans smashed the windows of his public house at Spring Hill.

Season 1892-3 saw Villa in fourth place in the table and out of the FA Cup in the first round when Darwen beat them 5-4 in a thrilling tie in Lancashire. But just as Villa had been edging up that Football League table, they did not have to wait any longer for the title. In 1893-4 Aston Villa sat on top of the sixteen-club division for the first time to win the Football League Championship. They took the title six points ahead of runners-up Sunderland and scored eighty-four goals in just thirty matches. In the FA Cup, Villa might have reached the later stages but for appalling conditions at Sheffield Wednesday in the third round where they lost 3-2 in a bog, only three days after winning a replay on an ice-rink of a pitch against Sunderland at Perry Barr.

The following season the positions had been reversed. In 1894-5 Villa slipped off the top of the table and ended in third place, eight points behind the champions Sunderland and three behind runners-up Everton. But they reached the FA Cup final for the third time in their short history and won the trophy for the second time. Incredibly, their opponents on each occasion had been West Brom. The Villa team had again undergone major surgery. Tom Wilkes played in goal and his full-backs were Howard Spencer and Jim Welford. Devey moved over to centre-forward to allow Bob Chatt to come into the inside berth and on the left-wing Steve Smith teamed up with Dennis Hodgetts. Smith came from Cannock Chase and along with Spencer would win full international honours in the England team.

Villa's first round match was against Derby County at Perry Barr and that was won 2-1; Newcastle United were thrashed 7-1 and Nottingham Forest 6-2, and Villa were through to the semi-finals where they met Sunderland at Blackburn. Villa had already drawn 4-4 in a League game at Sunderland, although the Wearsiders later inflicted Villa's only home defeat of the season, and they took the field at Blackburn full of confidence. In a tight semi-final Villa squeezed home 2-1 and a third final appearance against the Throstles at Crystal Palace. The crowd which jammed into the south London ground was a record of over 42,000 — and yet over half of them missed the winning goal. It was scored within thirty seconds of the kick-off when Athersmith's centre was shot goalwards by Chatt, Albion's Joe Reader only half cleared, and the ball cannoned off John Devey's knee for a sensational start. Albion battled away but it was to no avail and the FA Cup came to Perry Barr yet again.

Once more Villa exchanged trophies in 1895-6 when they were knocked out of the FA Cup 4-2 at Derby in the first round, but went on to take the First Division Championship once again, this time finishing four points clear of runners-up Derby. But before they had officially lost the FA Cup on the field, Villa had already lost the actual silver trophy, which was in fact a comparatively small goblet weighing only

nineteen ounces. Villa put the cup on show in the window of William Shillcock, a football boot manufacturer of 73 Newtown Row. On the night of 11-12 September 1895 somebody stole it. There have been many theories — including the sensational 'confession' of an 83-year-old man in 1958 — but the cup was never found and Villa were fined £25 by the FA (although they had wisely insured the trophy for £200). Perhaps it was as well that they were knocked out so quickly, once the competition proper got underway — there would have been few volunteers to look after a new FA Cup!

Season 1896-7 was *the* season for Aston Villa —the season in which the club won both the FA Cup and the First Division championship, the last side to achieve this feat until the Spurs team of 1960-1. Towards the end of that season, Aston Villa also moved to the ground which was to become known through the football world as Villa Park. New players were also arriving at the club, not least of which was Jimmy Crabtree, a Scottish international full-back who joined Villa from Burnley. To further strengthen the defence, Villa also signed the Grimsby Town goalkeeper Jimmy Whitehouse for £200 — then a record transfer fee for a goalkeeper.

One player going in an opposite direction was Dennis Hodgetts who joined Villa's Birmingham rivals Small Heath and thus missed being part of an almost unique football team when his old club won the double. Villa also paid Small Heath £100 plus the proceeds of a testimonial game when inside-forward Fred Wheldon came to Perry Barr. With these and other signings, Aston Villa began to rewrite soccer's record book.

Let us take their League Championship first. Villa romped away with the title until their nearest rivals Sheffield United were eleven points adrift when the final games had been played. The top of the 1896-7 First Division looked like this, Villa having already made sure of the title before they went to the Crystal Palace for the FA Cup final:

		P	W	D	L	F	A	Pts
1	Aston Villa	30	21	5	4	73	38	47
2	Sheffield Utd	30	13	10	7	42	29	36
3	Derby County	30	16	4	10	70	50	36
4	Preston	30	11	12	7	55	40	34
5	Liverpool	30	12	9	9	46	38	33
6	Wednesday	30	10	11	9	42	37	31

In the cup first round Villa beat Newcastle United 5-1 at home (also appearing in that first round draw were such long-forgotten names as Burton Town, Burton Swifts, Stockton and Glossop North End). Notts County came to Perry Barr for the second round and lost 2-1 and after a third round tie against Preston which went to three games before Villa won the second replay.

Liverpool at Bramall Lane was their semi-final
obstacle. The tie was one-sided as Villa powered to a
3-0 win at the home of Sheffield United and into
their fourth final. At last, they had different
opponents, for Everton had beaten Derby County in
the other semi-final at Stoke, Liverpool thus missing
out on what would have been an historic all-
Merseyside final. An official estimate put the final
attendance at 65,024 and about 20,000 of those must
have come from Birmingham. They witnessed one of
the most entertaining of all FA Cup finals with five
goals being scored in a period of little more than half-
an hour.

After both sides had started brightly, Villa took
the lead after eighteen minutes. Devey gave John
Campbell a perfectly measured through-ball and the
centre-forward cracked a magnificent shot past
Menham in the Everton goal. But the Merseysiders
were not to be outdone and within a short space of
time it was the sky blue shirts of Everton who were
doing a victory jig. First Bell combined with Hartley
before giving Whitehouse no chance, to make it 1-1;
then Cowan conceded a free-kick and Boyle planted
it past Whitehouse to give Everton the lead. Ten
minutes later Villa were level again when Crabtree
dropped a free-kick into the path of Wheldon who
made the score 2-2. With the crowd still buzzing
from this sensational spate of scoring, Villa won a
corner and when the ball came over from the

righthand flag, Crabtree took full advantage of
Everton's slack marking to run in and head the
winner. In the second half both sides continued to
thrill the crowd but there were no more goals and the
referee ended the game. Aston Villa were double
champions.

On Easter Saturday, 17 April 1897 — a cold, wet
day — Aston Villa officially opened what was to
become Villa Park, although then it was still known
as Aston Lower Grounds. The first visitors were
Blackburn Rovers in a special friendly game to mark
the occasion and Villa won 3-0, John Campbell
scoring the first-ever goal on the new ground.

The grounds had been a kind of pleasure park for
working people and Villa's early matches had
sometimes been played on the adjoining meadow
before they moved to Perry Barr. When the new
ground was completed it had a stand which seated
5,500 fans, a further 4,500 standing in front. A
further 8,000 could find accommodation on the
Trinity Road side of the stadium, and the rest had to
be content with open terraces. A concrete cycle track
ran round the pitch. Frederick Rinder and Charles
Johnstone did the early work in negotiating a lease
from the owners, Flowers Brewery, and it ran for 21
years at a starting rate of £250 per annum. By 1911,
Villa were in a position to buy the freehold at about
five shilling a yard, together with further land from

*Aston Villa. Double winners 1896-7. Pictured with the FA
Cup and Football League Championship trophy are, back
row, left to right: G. B. Ramsey (secretary), J. Grierson
(trainer), H. Spencer, J. Whitehouse, J. Margoschis
(chairman), A. Evans, J. Crabtree, J. Lees (director), C.
Johnstone (director). Front row: V. Jones (director),
James Cowan, C. Athersmith, J. Campbell, J. Devey
(captain), F. Wheldon, John Cowan, J. Reynolds, F. W.
Rinder (director).*

Ansells Brewery. Villa were well on the way to owning a stadium which would compare with the best in the world and only World War I prevented them from developing the stadium into one which would have held a massive 130,000 people. It was sad, however, that the famous old Perry Barr ground was to close. On Good Friday, 1897 Villa reserves met Shrewsbury Town in a Birmingham League game — it was to be the last match ever played at the grand old venue.

Aston Villa were to add two more FA Cup wins and three First Division Championships to their record before World War I intervened and closed down soccer for the duration. During that period of some eighteen years between the move to Villa Park and the war, there were to be many more famous names associated with the legendary claret and blue shirt of the club which had become one of the greatest names in football.

Villa took the First Division titles in successive seasons in 1898-99 and 1899-1900, although some bizarre incidents surrounded the period. Apart from being fined £50 for alleged irregularities over the signing of goalkeeper Bill George, a soldier who was stationed in Wiltshire, Villa were also involved in a match in November 1898 which will go down as one of the silliest decisions ever made by the Football League. With almost eighty minutes gone in the game against Wednesday at Sheffield, Villa were losing 3-1 when the referee ended the game due to bad light. The League ordered that the remaining ten minutes be played *four months later* and Villa made the trek back to Yorkshire for the farce which saw Wednesday score another goal to win 4-1.

That season Villa contested the title with Liverpool, finally finishing two points clear of the Merseysiders by beating them in the very last game of the season at Villa Park before over 41,000 fans who saw John Devey (2), Fred Wheldon (2) and Jim Crabtree complete a resounding five goal win. The top of the table was:

	P	W	D	L	F	A	Pts
1 Aston Villa	34	19	7	8	76	40	45
2 Liverpool	34	19	5	10	49	33	43
3 Burnley	34	15	9	10	45	47	39

Liverpool dropped right out of the race the following season but Villa kept right on until they completed their fifth First Division Championship win in seven consecutive seasons, this time two points ahead of Sheffield United in this table:

	P	W	D	L	F	A	Pts
1 Aston Villa	34	22	6	6	77	35	50
2 Sheffield Utd	34	18	12	4	63	33	48
3 Sunderland	34	19	3	12	50	35	41

Villa, themselves, dropped down the table in 1900-01, finishing in fifteenth place and avoiding relegation by just five points, but they did reach the FA Cup semi-finals and drew 2-2 with Sheffield United at Nottingham before losing the replay 3-0 at Derby. In the quarter-finals, Villa had been held to a goalless draw by Small Heath, then of the Second Division, before winning the replay at Villa Park 1-0. Small Heath had doubled the admission price to one shilling for their home tie with the result that many Villa fans stayed away.

Season 1902-03 saw Villa back near the top of the First Division when they finished runners-up behind Wednesday who scraped to the title by just one point; and when Villa also reached the semi-final of the FA Cup before losing 3-0 to the eventual winners, Bury, it was felt at Villa Park that the lapses of the previous two years were only temporary affairs. Sure enough, in 1904-05, Villa were back in the cup final. Villa also found a hero in that season. Harry Hampton joined the club from Wellington Town as a fiery centre-forward and, as Villa marched towards another cup final, Hampton came to full prominence. The cup trail started with a 5-1 win over Leicester Fosse at Villa Park; there followed a 3-2 win over Bury, also at home, and then in the quarter-finals Villa demolished Fulham 5-0 in Birmingham. Safely into the semi-finals, Villa found the going much tougher against Everton, the eventual First Division runners-up, and after drawing 1-1 at Stoke, Villa finally edged their way through 2-1 at Nottingham to face an even more daunting task in the final itself — Newcastle United, the League Champions. But they need not have worried. In the third minute Hampton gave Villa the lead with a superb goal and, although Villa lost the initiative for a period, Hampton made it 2-0 fifteen minutes from time and Villa had won the cup for the fourth time.

Aston Villa beat Newcastle United 2-0 in the 1905 FA Cup final. Back row left to right: G. Ramsey (Secretary), F. Miles, H. Toney (director), H. Spencer (captain), F. W. Rinder (chairman), W. George, J. Devey (director), J. Grierson (trainer). Middle row: V. Jones (director), W. Brawn, W. Garratty, H. Hampton, J. Bache, A. Hall, J. Lees (director). Front row: J. Pearson, A. Leake, J. Windmill.

Aston Villa players who helped the club to the First Division Championship in 1909-10. It was Villa's sixth title — and their last.

In 1907-08 Villa became First Division runners up, although finishing well behind the champions Manchester United, and this paved the way for the sixth title in 1909-10. Villa lost only eight matches and were unbeaten at home, scoring eighty-four goals in thirty-eight matches — a fine striking rate even in those days. Manchester United were hammered 7-1, Woolwich Arsenal 5-1, and Sheffield Wednesday also suffered a five goal defeat. Villa also smashed six goals past Derby in a second round FA Cup-tie before themselves losing 2-1 to Manchester City at Villa Park. This was to be the last time — at least for the moment — that Villa would win the First Division title, all of their six wins coming in the first thirty-five years of the club's existence, although they were to finish runners-up three more times before 1914.

Villa made one more FA Cup final appearance before World War I when they won the trophy for the fifth time, beating Sunderland 1-0 at the Crystal Palace in 1913. By the time they had reached the semi-final that year, Villa had scored eighteen goals in four ties against Derby (3-1), West Ham (5-0), Crystal Palace (5-0) and Bradford (5-0). In the semi-final Villa met Oldham at Blackburn and beat them 1-0, while Sunderland scraped through 3-2 against Burnley after the first game had ended 0-0.

There were two survivors of Villa's last FA Cup final appearance in 1905 — Harry Hampton and Joe Bache. Hampton had in fact scored the only goal of England's win over Scotland in 1913 when he bundled the Scottish goalkeeper over the line. In Villa's goal for the final against Sunderland — the Wearsiders' first appearance in a cup final — was the legendary Sam Hardy who had taken over from Billy George, and who had already won ten England caps before he joined Villa from Liverpool.

It was an FA Cup final with a difference for the participants were also first and second in the First Division — Sunderland the eventual champions and Villa runners-up, four points behind. The occasion was reflected by the size of the crowd which at 120,081 was a record attendance, and although the match was not an epic, there was plenty of good football to please the paying spectators. Villa should have taken the lead in the fifteenth minute when they were awarded a penalty but Wallace was overcome by the tension and shot wide. Then Sam Hardy was carried off with a knee injury and Jimmy Harrop took his place in goal with Hampton moving back to centre-half. Eventually Hardy returned and Villa regained their composure, until late in the game they scored the only goal. Wallace took a low corner and Barber headed it home. Sunderland had fielded such stars as Charlie Buchan, who combined with Cuggy and Mordue to form one of the best right-wing triangles of the day, but they had been only secondbest in the 1913 FA Cup final.

Villa finished runners-up in the First Division in 1913-14 and reached the semi-finals of the cup again before losing 2-0 to Liverpool at White Hart Lane. The following season was football's last until peace was restored and Villa slipped to thirteenth place in the table and allowed Manchester City to beat them 1-0 in the second round of the cup. Then the lights went out and Aston Villa footballers went to do

> **On the Wednesday following their 1913 FA Cup defeat of Sunderland, Villa met the Wearsiders in a vital League match at Villa Park before what was then a record midweek attendance of 53,000. Sunderland managed a 1-1 draw to take the title and kill Villa's hopes of another double.**

battle of a different kind. Since their formation in 1874 Villa had won the FA Cup five times in six finals, and taken the First Division Championship six times, finishing runners-up a further six. It was an incredible performance and ensured that the name of Aston Villa Football Club would live forever, no matter what happened after the war. Players like those already mentioned, teamed up with others like Billy Garratty, Alec Leake, Albert Hall, Chris Buckley and Clem Stephenson, to become as much to the young boys of Birmingham then, as the present-day heroes in claret and blue.

BETWEEN TWO WARS

When football resumed for the 1919-20 season the Football League arranged the programme so that the clubs played each other on succeeding weeks — for instance, Villa would be at home to West Brom one week and then away at the Hawthorns the next. It was an arrangement which suited West Brom better than it did Villa for, while the Throstles went on to become First Division Champions, Villa had to wait until the first Saturday in October for their first League win — a 1-0 win over Bradford — and by the middle of the month they were firmly bedded at the foot of the table with just three points from ten games.

But a transformation was on the way and it coincided with the signing of a player who was to become a major part of the Aston Villa story between the wars. Frank Barson, the Barnsley centre-half, joined Villa in October 1919 and made his debut at Middlesbrough when Villa scored a sensational 4-1 win to begin their fight back. Barson was joined at Villa by an inside-forward called Billy Kirton who came to the club from Leeds City, the side kicked out of the Football League for alleged irregularities. Both men were to play a big part in Villa's drive that season when they went on to win the FA Cup. Like most sides, Villa had lost several players to the war, although in Villa's case only Tommy Barber and Arthur Dobson, a young centre-half, had been killed in the fighting; but Bache, Halse and Lyons had left the club and that had left a big hole in the 1913 FA Cup-winning side. But with Barson, Kirton and another young player — Billy Walker — Villa were

rebuilding that side around men like Hardy, Weston, Harrop and Stephenson who were now veterans.

In January, with Villa now climbing slowly up the table, the FA Cup came around and in the first round Queen's Park Rangers came to Villa Park and were beaten 2-1. It was in that game that Walker made his debut. The son of George Walker, a Wolverhampton Wanderers defender, Billy Walker was set to become a great player, both at club and international level, and a great manager. When Villa fans first saw his dazzling performance in the cup game, they sensed that the club had signed a 'good 'un'.

Villa beat Manchester United at Old Trafford and Sunderland at Villa Park to reach the quarter-finals and a game at White Hart Lane where Spurs fullback, Tommy Clay, put through his own goal to send Villa into the semi-final against Chelsea at Bramall Lane. Chelsea had the added incentive of knowing that if they won, the FA Cup final would be on their own ground of Stamford Bridge. They did not have the opportunity of that advantage. Two goals from Billy Walker put Villa into their seventh final against Huddersfield Town, the team which would finish Second Division runners-up that season. Harold Edgley missed that final. Three weeks before the game he broke his leg against Chelsea in a League match at — Stamford Bridge! Villa would have been forgiven for thinking that a cup hoodoo had overtaken them as they ran out to take on Huddersfield on the same pitch on which their winger had suffered his tragic accident. Town were confident of a unique double of FA cup and Second Division championship. In eight League matches up to the final, the Yorkshiremen took fourteen points. However, the double eluded them as Spurs took the title and Villa lifted the FA Cup.

Villa went into the game with a side naturally much changed from the one which contested the 1913 final. Besides the changes already mentioned, Harrop was injured before the final and the Villa skipper had to hand over the captaincy to Andy Ducat, the wing-half who had joined Villa from Woolwich Arsenal in 1912 and who played both soccer and cricket for England. Another addition to the Villa side was left-half Frank Moss, the only Aston-born player in the team. Moss had signed for Villa in 1914 but had to wait until the 1920 FA Cup final for a debut more in keeping with a boy's comic hero.

Only 50,000 watched the first post-war final, many believing that the crowd would be so great that they would not stand a chance of gaining admittance. With record receipts of almost £10,000, one wonders what receipts would have been with a full house. For ninety minutes the two sides battled without a goal being scored and for the first time, an FA Cup final went into extra-time. In the seventh minute of that extra-time, Villa scored the only goal of the game —

Villa beat Huddersfield Town 1–0 after extra-time in the 1920 FA Cup final: Back row left to right: G. Ramsey (secretary), Smart, P. Bate (director), F. W. Rinder (chairman), Hardy, Miles, Moss, H. Spencer (director). Middle row: J. Devey (director), Kirton, Ducat, Walker, Stephenson, J. Jones (director). Front row: Wallace, Barson, Weston, Dorrell.

and what a lucky goal it was too. Dorrell took a corner and Kirton went up for it with the Huddersfield goalkeeper and their centre-half. Kirton got his head to the ball and nodded it goalwards where it flew off Wilson (Town's pivot) and past Mutch in the Huddersfield goal to take the FA Cup to Villa Park for the sixth time in seven finals.

It was a fluke of a goal and one not worthy of an FA Cup final, but Villa had the edge on the day and at least it served to ensure that justice was done, although there were many Yorkshiremen who felt otherwise. It was a particularly significant moment for Villa secretary Billy Smith. It was Smith who had signed Tommy Barber, the man who headed the Villa winner in the 1913 final. Now his latest signing, Billy Kirton, had done likewise.

Although Villa were to reach another FA Cup final before a second war was declared, and despite the fact that they would finish First Division runners-up twice in that period, the writing was on the wall for the club which had dominated the early history of English soccer. Even the arrival of such famous names as 'Pongo' Waring, Eric Houghton and Jimmy Gibson would not alter the fact that the Villa machine was running out of steam and that there would soon be new teams like Bolton, Huddersfield and Arsenal coming up to take over the Villa place as League and Cup experts.

In 1920-1 Villa finished tenth in the First Division and went out of the FA Cup in the quarter-finals when Spurs, the eventual winners, beat them 1–0 at White Hart Lane; the following season Villa had climbed up to fifth place in the League and again reached the FA Cup quarter-finals, this time losing 4–3 to Notts County at Villa Park after a 2–2 draw at Meadow Lane. In 1922-3 Villa went out of the cup as early as the first round when Blackburn Rovers won 1–0 at Villa Park, although Villa were by now

without Frank Barson who had signed for Manchester United. Barson's replacement in the Villa team for that cup defeat by Blackburn was Tom Ball. Sadly, Ball was to meet a violent death when he was stabbed after an argument.

In 1923-4 Villa reached their eighth FA Cup final. The first round sent them to Ashington, then of the Third Division (North), where they duly won 5–1. In the second round they beat Swansea Town 2–0 at Vetch Field, and in the third, Leeds United visited Villa Park and lost 3–0. In the quarter-finals, West Brom had home advantage but Villa won the game at the Hawthorns 2–0 and advanced once more into the semi-finals, where they trounced Burnley 3–0 and so looked forward to Newcastle United at Wembley — only the second time that the game had been played at this famous stadium. Five days before the final, Newcastle came to Villa Park for an Easter holiday First Division match. A huge crowd packed the ground for a rehearsal of the FA Cup final but they were bitterly disappointed. United fielded only one player who was to play at Wembley and Villa won 6–1, while the Football League fined Newcastle the considerable sum of £750 for that and other offences concerning playing weakened sides before the final.

Frank Moss captained Villa as the teams walked out to be presented to the Duke of York in pouring

Three of Villa's most distingushed players seen here in their days as directors at Villa Park: Left to right: Howard Spencer, Howard Vaughton and John Devey.

Dickie York, a former Royal Flying Corps officer in the 1914-18 war, who signed for Villa in 1919 and had a brilliant career as a right winger. He won two England caps against Scotland and played for Villa in the 1924 FA Cup final.

rain. In the Villa goal Tommy Jackson had succeeded Sam Hardy; Clem Stephenson had joined Huddersfield with whom he won an FA Cupwinners medal in 1922; Dickie York played on the right wing and had already played for England; George Blackburn replaced Jimmy Harrop at left-half; and Dr Victor Milne, a sturdy Scottish centre-half, became the first Scot to play in an FA Cup final for Aston Villa since 1897. Although Villa attacked furiously and hit the Newcastle woodwork twice, they could not find the back of the net and with five minutes to play, extra-time seemed inevitable. But then Newcastle struck — and struck again. First Harris took a clearance from Jackson — a clearance which both Villa backs could have snapped up —and fired the ball back past the unfortunate Villa goalkeeper; then Seymour ran through the Villa defence without having to evade one tackle and made

> **Villa lost the 1924 FA Cup to Newcastle United with this team: T. Jackson; T. Smart, T. Mort; F. Moss, Dr V. Milne, G. Blackburn; R. York, W. Kirton, L. Capewell, W. H. Walker, A. Dorell.**

it 2–0 via the underside of the Villa crossbar. The cup went to Newcastle and it would be thirty-three years before Aston Villa played in another final.

The next twelve years were a curious mixture of hope and despair for Villa fans. In the season immediately following that Wembley defeat, they were to see their team knocked out of the cup in the third round and finish fifteenth in the First Division, a record which was similarly matched for the next few seasons until 1928-9 when Villa climbed to third place in the table and fought through to the FA Cup semi-finals. There were highlights in between those years — like Villa's 10–0 win over Burnley at Villa Park on the opening day of the 1925-6 season, although that result was tempered by the news that Villa owed £55,000 to the bank and various creditors. Villa also introduced two new players to their side — 'Pongo' Waring and Eric Houghton — and both were to become synonymous with the name of Aston Villa FC. Houghton signed in August 1927 from a Lincolnshire village side and became a great Villa star; Waring came in February 1928 as a free-scoring forward from Tranmere Rovers.

In the third round of the 1928-9 cup Villa hammered Cardiff City 6–1 and although Clapton

Orient's giant goalkeeper Arthur Wood managed to help his team to a 0–0 draw in the fourth round at Villa Park, even his considerable frame could not prevent Villa winning 8–0 in the replay in London. Reading lost 3–1 in Berkshire in the fifth round and in the quarter-finals Villa defeated Arsenal 1–0 at Villa Park. 'Pongo' Waring added the only goal of this match to the hat-trick he had scored at Clapton and the two he had netted at Reading. Arsenal had some kind of revenge when Villa went to Highbury for the semi-final against Portsmouth and lost 1–0 to a Jack Smith penalty.

> **When 'Pongo' Waring made his reserve team debut for Aston Villa against Birmingham City, over 23,000 turned up for the game and saw Waring score a hat-trick.**

The following season of 1929-30 saw Aston Villa into the quarter-finals. Along the way they had beaten near-neighbours Walsall 3–1 when a record gate of 74,600 all but burst the seams of Villa Park. The game is also memorable for the fact that after its conclusion, Villa signed the Walsall goalkeeper Fred Biddlestone who went on to serve Villa well,

Jimmy Gibson, Partick Thistle's brilliant Scottish international wing-half who signed for Villa in April 1927. Gibson was a member of the club's superb half-back line of the mid-1930s.

Aston Villa 1929-30. Back row, left to right: Kingdon, Smart, Olney, Talbot, Tate, H. Gooch (trainer), Gibson. Front row: York, Beresford, Walker, Brown, Chester, Mort. George Brown signed from Huddersfield and scored some great goals for Villa including five against Leicester City in January 1932 when Villa won 8-3.

although he was often left out of the side in favour of other goalkeepers, only to come fighting back each time. In the last eight of the 1929-30 cup, Villa met Huddersfield Town who beat them 2-1 at Villa Park on their way to Wembley.

The 1930s started with anything but a depression for Aston Villa. In three seasons they finished second, fifth and second in the First Division and in the following season, 1933-4, they reached the FA Cup semi-finals again. It was Villa's thirteenth appearance in the last-but-one hurdle to the cup and the fans were happy enough even though Villa eventually lost the chance of a Wembley appearance when Manchester City beat them 6-1 at Huddersfield. But Villa's league position should have given them cause for concern. While gaining some cup glory, Villa had been sliding down the First Division and at the end of that season they were in thirteenth place, losing sixteen matches and conceding seventy-five goals. It was a long way from the previous season's triumphs of runners-up position when they had finished just four points behind the champions, Arsenal. But in 1933-4 it was obvious that Villa's troubles lay in their defence and when Manchester City whipped six goals past them in the semi-final, the truth had to be faced. Late in that season Villa appointed their first team manager, Jimmy McMullan, then manager of Oldham Athletic and a former Manchester City and Scotland wing-half.

McMullan began to add players to the Villa staff he had inherited. One of them was a young forward called Frank Broome who came from Berkhamstead Town and soon made his mark, scoring six goals against Moor Green in a Birmingham Combination game. McMullan also bought Jimmy McLuckie, the Scottish international wing-half, from his old club, and also signed Jimmy Allen from Portsmouth for a record fee of £10,500. Allen, a classic 'stopper' type of centre-half, came in for some criticism from Villa Park fans who were used to a more attacking kind of centre-half. Despite these signings, and despite the brilliance of players like Houghton (who missed a penalty in his debut against Leeds in January 1930), George Cummings, Dai Astley and Ronnie Dix, Villa were on the downward path and in 1935-6 the

Ernie 'Mush' Callaghan. He signed for Villa from Atherstone Town in 1930 but had to wait until January 1933 for his debut in the FA Cup third round replay with Bradford City at Villa Park. Callaghan was a fine full-back and centre-half and in 1942 he won the BEM for bravery during the Birmingham blitz.

club reached its nadir. After forty-eight years of First Division soccer, Aston Villa were relegated to the Second Division. They finished next-to-bottom of the table, two points ahead of Blackburn, and conceded 110 goals, fifty-six of them at Villa Park where even Blackburn won 4–2 on the very last day of a dreadful season.

Goals galore were piled past the Villa defence and on 14 December 1935, Arsenal's Ted Drake had eight shots at the Villa goal and scored with seven of them as Arsenal won 7–1. Never before, or since, has a player scored so many goals on an opponent's ground in the Football League. West Brom and Grimsby Town each scored six times at Villa Park and manager McMullan resigned the job during October. Amazingly, Villa managed to beat both the eventual champions, Sunderland, and the runners-up Derby County at Roker Park and the Baseball Ground. But when the season ended, Villa fans had to face the fact that they would be watching Second Division soccer in 1936-7. Money had been spent on

		P	W	D	L	F	A	Pts
18	West Brom	42	16	6	20	89	88	38
19	Liverpool	42	13	12	17	60	64	38
20	Sheff Wed	42	13	12	17	63	77	38
21	Aston Villa	42	13	9	20	81	110	35
22	Blackburn	42	12	9	21	55	96	33

1935-6 was a black season for Villa as they went into the Second Division for the first time. The foot of the table looked like this:

new players but the plain truth was that Aston Villa had no Divine Right to success, despite their impeccable record. Another boardroom upheaval preceded the season and the new regime secured the signature of Jimmy Hogan as team manager. A Lancashire lad who had played with Fulham, Swindon and Bolton, Hogan had made his name as a coach in Austria and Hungary and he set about the task of returning Aston Villa to the First Division. In their first season in the Second Division, Villa finished in ninth position as Hogan began to sort out the team. Several players either retired or were transferred, amongst them the legendary 'Pongo' Waring.

The season started in fine style with ten points from the first six games including a 5–1 win over Bradford City at Villa Park. Former Liverpool

player Gordon Hodgson scored a hat-trick and Villa Park fans looked forward to an early return to the First Division. But slowly it dawned on them that it would not be that easy to return to the top flight straight away. Fulham won at Villa Park and Doncaster took both points at Belle Vue. When Sheffield United beat Villa 5–1 at Bramall Lane and Leicester won 3–1 at Villa Park in early December, it was even more obvious. At the end of the campaign Villa had dropped sixteen points at home, their illusions of a top-two place finally shattered over the Easter holiday when Newcastle won 2–0 at Villa Park on Easter Tuesday.

Villa fans had not got to wait long for First Division soccer to return to their beloved Villa Park, however. In 1937-8 Villa romped away with the Second Division title, finishing four points ahead of Manchester United. They also finished the season with a flourish when they won through to the semi-final of the FA Cup. In the League, it was Villa's defence that took the honours. The forwards managed only seventy-three goals but Villa conceded only thirty-five. Villa took up the challenge for the title on New Year's Day 1938 when a 1–1 draw at West Ham put them on top of the table for the first time. They stayed there until February and then fought it out with Manchester United, Sheffield United and Coventry before clinching the Championship with a draw at Bramall Lane on 9 April. Their two games with Coventry produced record gates for both clubs as far as League matches were concerned — 68,029 at Villa Park in October, and 44,930 at Highfield Road in March.

New manager Jimmy Hogan shows the Villa players a few tricks at the start of 1936-7.

In the FA Cup, too, attendance records fell. When Villa beat Manchester City 3–2 in the sixth round on 5 March 1938, 75,000 paid over £5,500 into the Villa Park turnstiles. Villa also found a new star in centre-forward Fred Shell. Shell joined Villa from Ford Sports of Dagenham in May 1937 and on his second appearance for the club, against Stockport County on 11 December 1937, he scored a hat-trick in a 7–1 win; he linked up with Frank Broome to provide a fearsome striking force for the rest of that season. Although Villa lost the FA Cup semi-final, 2–1 to Preston at Bramall Lane, they finished the season in magnificent style. After that goalless draw at Sheffield United which virtually gave them the title, they rounded off the season with wins over Swansea Town at Villa Park (4–0), Stockport, Bradford and Norwich. Villa were back in the First Division.

Villa's staff for 1939-40 — 'the season-that-never-was'. Back row left to right: H. Bourne (trainer), Massie, Callaghan, Cummings, Allen, Biddleston, Starling, Beeson, Iverson, Gardner, J. Hogan (manager). Front row: C. Buckley (director), Martin, J. Broughton (director), Griffiths, F. Normansell (chairman), Phillips, F. Rinder (vice-chairman), Broome, J. Riley (director). On ground: Pritty, Owen, Houghton, Jones, Cobley, Maund, Haycock.

After two seasons of Second Division football Villa were back amongst the elite. The top of the 1937-8 Second Division finished as follows:

	P	W	D	L	F	A	Pts
1 Aston Villa	42	25	7	10	73	35	57
2 Man Utd	42	22	9	11	82	50	53
3 Sheff Utd	42	22	9	11	73	56	53
4 Coventry C	42	20	12	10	66	45	52

There was to be only one season of First Division soccer, however, before World War II intervened (Villa players had refused to emulate the England team and give the Nazi salute when they made a close-season tour to Germany in the summer of 1938). In that one season, Villa finished twelfth in the table and reached the fourth round of the FA Cup before losing 2–0 to Preston North End. On Christmas Day, 1938, Frederick Rinder died. In his eighties, Rinder had devoted his life to football and to Villa. He was senior vice-president of the Football Association at his death. Villa had played just three matches in the 1939-40 season when war was declared. On the last Saturday of peace, Jack Nicholas's penalty beat them at Derby's Baseball Ground before the League programme was curtailed. Like all other sides, Villa played in wartime competitions, often with 'guest' players from whichever servicemen happened to be stationed near Villa Park at the time. In 1944 they won the Football League (North) War Cup by beating Blackpool. It was all a far cry from the days of pre-war soccer. Like the previous conflict, World War II changed the lives of thousands of sportsmen and many, including some Villa players, were too old to continue when peace came. Others had six years taken out of the middle of their careers and when football started up again for the 1945-6 FA Cup

(played for the first and only time on a two-legged basis) soccer teams in the Football League were a curious mixture of ageing skill and raw experience.

In that first season, the Football League was divided into two premier sections of Leagues North and South, and Black Country soccer fans enjoyed the fact that Birmingham won League South with Villa coming second. Harry Parkes had joined the club from Boldmere St Michael's in 1939 and he made an immediate impact. Other players in the 'new' Villa team were Alex Massie who had played before the war and was soon to take over as team manager, Vic Potts, George Edwards who scored thirty-nine goals in 1945-6, and stalwarts like 'Mush' Callaghan, Frank Broome and Eric Houghton.

PEACE — AND SOME GREAT PLAYERS

In the strangely-structured FA Cup, Villa beat Coventry, Millwall and Chelsea on aggregate to reach the quarter-finals, having disposed of Millwall 9–1 at Villa Park in their second-leg tie, with Broome scoring a hat-trick. Then Villa faced Derby County in the last eight and the first-leg was played at Villa Park. The war had left Derby with a great side. At inside-forward they had those two legends, Raich Carter and Peter Doherty while Sammy Crooks and 'Dally' Duncan sped down the wings. Yet with five minutes of the first-leg remaining, Villa were leading 3–2. It looked a useful win but when Duncan centred the ball high over the Villa defence, Doherty jumped to head the equaliser. Before Villa could settle down, Crooks nipped in for the winner. When the sides met at the Baseball Ground, Broome put Villa in front again but Carter levelled the scores and so put Derby in front on aggregate. The Rams went on to win the FA Cup.

For the remainder of the 1940s, Villa never got beyond the fourth round of the competition, losing to Burnley (3rd round 1946-7); Manchester United (3rd round 1947-8); Cardiff (4th round 1948-9); and Middlesbrough (3rd round 1949-50 after two replays). In the First Division they could finish no higher than sixth (in 1947-8) and no lower than twelfth (1949-50). Yet there was a new genre of Aston Villa footballer arriving on the scene. Villa's first First Division game for seven years was on 31 August 1946 when 50,000 fans saw them play Middlesbrough with a team that included only Cummings, Callaghan and Broome of the side which played the previous First Division fixture against Derby on 2 September 1939. And before long there would be more new arrivals. Dickie Dorsett came from Wolverhampton Wanderers as a skilful wing-half or inside-forward; Johnny Dixon from Newcastle United was in the side that lost to Middlesbrough and a Wilf Mannion goal; fiery Welsh centre-forward Trevor Ford came from Swansea for £9,500; England international winger Leslie Smith had already signed from Brentford; Ivor Powell, the talented Welsh international inside-forward came from Queen's Park Rangers in 1948 after eleven seasons at Loftus Road.

Two matches stand out in that period of Aston Villa's story. In the third round of the 1947-8 FA Cup, Villa were drawn at home to Manchester United. After thirteen-and-a-half seconds George Edwards completed a four-man Villa move to give them a sensational lead without a United player having touched the ball. But United fought back and after thirty minutes they led 3–1 through Jack Rowley, Johnny Morris and Rowley again. At half-time Morris and Delaney had made it 5–1 and Villa looked dead.

Vic Potts made the right-back position his own in the years immediately following World War II.

But when Jack Crompton failed to gather Edwards's corner, Villa were back in the game and with twenty minutes to go Smith made it 5–3. Nine minutes from time Dorsett scored and with Villa looking for what would have been a sensational equaliser, United stole up field (though not before Ford had hit the bar) and from a corner Pearson made it 6–4. Ten goals had been scored in a superb game of soccer. It was a magnificent performance by both sides.

Leslie Smith, another of Villa's post-war stars.

Villa finished eighth in the First Division in 1946-7 — the club's first league campaign since 1939. Back row, left to right: Smith, Lowe, Wakeman, Martin, Starling, Rutherford, F. Moss, Parkes. Middle row: H. Bourne (trainer), Edwards, Dorsett, Cummings, Iverson, Potts, A. Massie (manager). Front row: Ashton, Ford, Dixon, Moss, Callaghan.

Aston Villa's team which lost 6-4 to Manchester United in the FA Cup third round of 1947-8 was: Jones; Potts, Parkes; Dorsett, Moss (F), Lowe; Edwards, Martin, Ford, Brown, Smith.

The other match was in the 1948-9 season. On New Year's Day 1949 Villa were bottom of the First Division with sixteen points from twenty-five games, having lost 5-2 at home to Blackpool. There followed a difficult third round FA Cup match with Bolton, and Villa managed a 1-1 draw at Villa Park, followed by a goalless draw on a dreadful Burnden Park pitch. The second replay was at Villa Park and Villa won that 2-1. Although they lost out to Cardiff in the next round, Villa had turned the corner. From the moment they had beaten Bolton, their League form changed and they took twenty-six points from their remaining seventeen games including wins over Arsenal, Huddersfield, Manchester United, Sheffield United, Manchester City, Everton, Preston, Charlton, Stoke and Birmingham to finish in tenth position. Much of the credit for the revival went to Ivor Powell who had signed the previous December and who had a tremendous impact on the Villa team.

Villa faced the 1950s with renewed confidence and that too was to be a decade in which more famous names came to Villa Park and the club's supporters found themselves donning claret and blue favours for a return trip to Wembley. There were, however, some dark clouds on the horizon.

'Sailor' Brown who laid on a 13½-second goal in the epic FA Cup tie against Manchester United in 1947-8. United finally triumphed 6-4 in a thrilling game.

Con Martin pulls on a Villa shirt for the first time watched by Smith, Mulraney and Lowe in September 1948. Although the Irish international signed as a full-back he played many games for Villa as an emergency goalkeeper.

Eddie Lowe, another Villa star in the traumatic cup-tie with Manchester United.

An informal Villa pose during 1949. Back row, left to right: Parkes, H. Bourne (trainer), Frank Moss junior, Edwards, Powell, Rutherford, Martin, Gibson. Front row: Smith, Vinal, Goffin, Dixon, Craddock.

Villa's Rutherford takes a high centre during the 2-1 win over Huddersfield Town in February 1950.

1950-1

Before the season had even started there was a shock for Villa fans when it was announced that manager Alex Massie had resigned. It was three months before Villa named Massie's successor — former Everton inside-forward, George Martin, who came to Villa Park from Newcastle United where he had been team boss. Martin had been at St James's Park since 1947 and he had also played with Hamilton, Hull, Middlesbrough and Luton Town. By the time Martin was installed at Villa Park it was clear that the club already had no hope of the First Division Championship and they did well to finish fifteenth in the table. The season was also marked by the departure of one fine player and the arrival of another.

On the outgoing scene, Trevor Ford left for Sunderland for the then record fee of £30,000; he had scored over fifty goals for Villa but in October 1950 his goal touch seemed to have eluded him and it was decided all round that a change of club would benefit both the fiery Welshman and Aston Villa. Coming into Villa Park was a young Irishman from Belfast, Danny Blanchflower. The quietly spoken graduate of St Andrew's University had first played for Glentoran before signing for Barnsley. Now he was a Villa player. Another player making his mark with Villa in the 1950-1 season was Stan Lynn, a hard-tackling full-back who had joined the club in March 1950. Just before Christmas, Villa bought a man to replace Ford. Dave Walshe, West Brom's Republic of Ireland centre-forward made the short journey across the Black Country.

Villa — with their youngest team since the war — struggled for survival for much of the season, hovering dangerously near the relegation zone for much of the time. Yet the season had begun in quite dramatic style with wins over West Bromwich Albion and Sunderland. But after that bright start, wins were few and far between. By the end of September Villa had only eight points and although they beat Newcastle soundly, they had to wait another month for their next win when they defeated Chelsea 4-2 at Villa Park.

Until Easter, Villa were always in danger of going down. Then they beat Wolves twice — the second match at Villa Park drawing a crowd of over 60,000. On the same day, West Brom beat Huddersfield, who were also contenders for the drop, and Villa then faced three matches against Sheffield Wednesday, Chelsea and Everton — all of them likely to fall from grace. It was clearly up to Villa to gain their own salvation. Villa did well enough. They beat Wednesday and Newcastle and earned a point from Stamford Bridge. But still the danger was not past and when Portsmouth drew 3-3 at Villa Park, Villa fans still had their worries. Then their team beat Everton 2-1 at Goodison and on the very last day of the season they managed a fine 6-2 win over Stoke City at Villa Park. It was Everton and Sheffield Wednesday who went down while Villa climbed to a healthy fifteenth place, although only five points separated them from twenty-first team, Wednesday.

In the third round of the cup Villa had beaten Burnley 2-0 at Villa Park but in the next round they

Aston Villa back row left to right: H. Bourne (trainer), Dixon, Parkes, Jones, Moss, Martin, Dorsett. Front row: Gibson, Ford, Powell, Craddock, Goffin.

Larry Canning, now a BBC commentator, heads towards the Middlesbrough goal at Villa Park in November 1950. Villa lost 1–0.

went down 3–1 to Wolves at Molineux. Nevertheless, it had been a satisfactory season, considering the awful consequences which seemed likely for much of the time. Martin had begun to settle his Aston Villa side down and Claret and Blue fans were looking forward to a big improvement in their club's fortunes the following season.

First Division results 1950-1

	H	A
Arsenal	1–1	1–2
Blackpool	0–3	1–1
Bolton	0–1	0–1
Burnley	3–2	0–2
Charlton	0–0	2–2
Chelsea	4–2	1–1
Derby	1–1	2–4
Everton	3–3	2–1
Fulham	3–0	1–2
Huddersfield	0–1	2–4
Liverpool	1–1	0–0
Manchester United	1–3	0–0
Middlesbrough	0–1	1–2
Newcastle	3–0	1–0
Portsmouth	3–3	3–3
Sheffield Wed	2–1	2–3
Stoke	6–2	0–1
Sunderland	3–1	3–3
Tottenham	2–3	2–3
West Brom	2–0	0–2
Wolves	1–0	3–2

Villa's Goffin is foiled by Manchester United goalkeeper Allen as Villa go down 3–1 in September 1950.

Final League Record

P	W	D	L	F	A	Pts	Pos
42	12	13	17	66	68	37	15th

FA Cup

Rnd 3	Burnley	(h)	2–0
Rnd 4	Wolves	(a)	1–3

1951-2

After their improved form in the second half of the previous season, Villa suffered a setback when after a good start to the season, they lost four games in succession, culminating in a 2-0 defeat at White Hart Lane by the previous season's champions Tottenham Hotspur. At this stage it seemed to the club's supporters that they would have to endure another year of uncertainty as Villa tried again to stave off relegation.

But there were better times on the way and Villa began to recover and to recapture that form which had seen them safely through 1950-1. By the end of 1951-2 Villa had climbed up to sixth place and were only ten points behind the champions Manchester United when the programme was completed. Indeed, Villa players almost qualified for talent money and only one point separated them from Portsmouth and Bolton, the fourth and fifth placed clubs. This drastic improvement had been achieved without a single big-money signing — the first time

since the war that no big-name player had pulled on a claret and blue shirt for the first time. But there were younger players who were gaining a recognised place in the Villa First Division side.

Stan Lynn held his place at full-back and partnered Harry Parkes, while behind the Villa back line, Con Martin played in goal for a time when Jones was injured. Martin had joined Villa as a full back but he had played in goal for his native Eire in 1946 during an injury crisis. Peter Aldis came through from Bourneville, and Derek Pace from Bloxwich Scouts. A gritty centre-forward, Pace made up for his lack of inches by being a rare battler in the penalty area.

Villa had one of their best-ever half-back lines during this period with the artistic Danny Blanchflower wearing the number four shirt in complete contrast to the powerful Dickie Dorsett on the other. Later in his illustrious career, Blanchflower was to form a similar combination with

Dave Walsh, Villa's Eire international centre-forward.

◀ *In April 1952 Villa hammered Chelsea 7–1 at Villa Park. Gibson heads the first goal following a corner.*

First Division results 1951-2

	H	A
Arsenal	1–0	1–2
Blackpool	4–0	3–0
Bolton	1–1	2–5
Burnley	4–1	1–2
Charlton	0–2	1–0
Chelsea	7–1	2–2
Derby	4–1	1–1
Fulham	4–1	2–2
Huddersfield	1–0	1–3
Liverpool	2–0	2–1
Manchester City	1–2	2–2
Manchester United	2–5	1–1
Middlesbrough	2–0	0–2
Newcastle	2–2	1–6
Portsmouth	2–0	0–2
Preston	3–2	2–2
Stoke	2–3	1–4
Sunderland	2–1	3–1
Tottenham	0–3	0–2
West Brom	2–0	2–1
Wolves	3–3	2–1

Final League Record

P	W	D	L	F	A	Pts	Pos
42	19	9	14	79	70	47	6th

FA Cup

Rnd 3	Newcastle	(a)	2–4

Dave Mackay at Tottenham. At centre-half in the Villa team of 1951-2, Frank Moss was now becoming as good a player as his father who had also given Villa yeoman service. Villa did have their problems at centre-forward where Dave Walshe failed to produce the form that had induced Villa to spend money on his transfer from West Brom; in the final analysis, this let in Johnny Dixon and he responded with twenty-six goals in the League, together with two in the FA Cup. Villa had some checkered results in this season. Manchester United beat them 5–2 at Villa Park, despite a brilliant display by Moss, and they also lost 5–2 at Bolton and 6–1 at Newcastle. On the credit side, we can look at a superb 7–1 win over Chelsea at Villa Park during the latter half of the season when Villa's forwards rattled up the club's highest score for some years. Burnley, Derby and

Fulham also felt the full weight of an on-song Aston Villa forward line as each of those clubs conceded four goals at Villa Park. Perhaps one of the club's best performances of the season, however, was a 3–0 win at Blackpool's Bloomfield Road. The steadying of the Villa defence meant that they finished the season with seventy goals against —sixteen of which had been conceded in only three games, which gives a better overall picture of the true improvement.

In the FA Cup, Villa fans were in for a disappointment. Newcastle United were on their way to Wembley to win the trophy from Arsenal and they started their run in the third round by beating Aston Villa at St James's Park. United won 4–2 but Villa were not disgraced. Johnny Dixon played well against his former team and he had the consolation of scoring both Villa's goals on his old hunting ground.

1952-3

Disastrous starts were by now a common feature of Aston Villa's story and the 1952-3 season was no exception. In their first ten games Villa managed only two victories although it must be said that the club suffered from a crop of injuries during that period when both Dixon and Thompson missed games. Dixon strained a ligament and then Thompson was bedevilled with a cartilage injury. Again Villa survived and although they finished lower than the previous season, they went to the sixth round of the FA Cup. As usual, one of the stalwarts of this revival was Harry Parkes. Parkes played his 400th League game for the club in October 1952 and he missed only two games all season. The rest of the defence rallied round and Villa conceded nine goals fewer than the previous campaign.

There were a few changes in personnel early in the season when Villa signed Norman Lockhart, the Irish international outside-left from Coventry City, and Derek Parsons, Wolves reserve team goalkeeper. Another new face to the Villa first team was Ken Roberts who made his debut on the right-wing and gave some displays which Villa found most reassuring after they had pinned their faith in the youngster from Crewe. An older face in a new role was that of Danny Blanchflower, who played several games at inside-forward when Villa were struggling through that injury crisis.

Although Blackpool gained revenge for Villa's win at Bloomfield Road the previous season, and won 5-1 at Villa Park, Villa also had their moments of goal-scoring glory. When Portsmouth made the journey from the south they were soundly whipped 6-0; and Liverpool, too, came a cropper at Villa Park when they went down 4-0. There was less joy for Villa at Charlton Athletic's sweeping Valley Ground where Charlton won 5-1; Manchester City also scored four goals against Villa at Maine Road. While Arsenal took the First Division Championship on goal average from Preston North End, Villa had to be content with the mid-table place that their early season lapses had brought.

In the FA Cup it was a slightly different story and for part of the cup programme, Villa fans entertained thoughts of Wembley. In the third round they saw Villa beat Middlesbrough 3-1 at Villa Park; after a goalless draw at Brentford in the next round, Walshe and Thompson gave Villa a 2-1 win in the replay; and in the fifth round it was the turn of Second Division Rotherham United to provide Villa with their passage into the quarter-finals. Rotherham had never got that far in the cup and 20,000 fans squeezed into their ramshackle Millmoor Ground to see Villa win 3-1. Dave Walshe scored twice and Billy Goffin once, as Villa negotiated an icy Millmoor pitch. Goffin was one of the heroes of Villa Park. A quick and direct player he endeared himself to the hearts of Villa fans. The sixth round brought Everton to Villa Park and the Merseysiders brought with them a large following of avid fans. The only goal of a rousing cup-tie was scored by Everton's fiery centre-forward Dave Hickson. Hickson enjoyed a similar reputation to that of Villa's ex-star Trevor Ford and his goal which put Everton into the semi-finals (where they lost 4-3 to Bolton Wanderers) was received with raptures by his many fans at Villa Park that day.

First Division results 1952-3

	H	A
Arsenal	1-2	1-3
Blackpool	1-5	1-1
Bolton	1-1	0-0
Burnley	2-0	0-1
Cardiff	2-0	2-1
Charlton	1-1	1-5
Chelsea	1-1	0-4
Derby	3-0	1-0
Liverpool	4-0	2-0
Manchester City	0-0	1-4
Manchester United	3-3	1-3
Middlesbrough	1-0	0-1
Newcastle	0-1	1-2
Portsmouth	6-0	1-1
Preston	1-0	3-1
Sheffield Wed	4-3	2-2
Stoke	1-1	4-1
Sunderland	3-0	2-2
Tottenham	0-3	1-1
West Brom	1-1	2-3
Wolves	0-1	1-2

Final League Record

P	W	D	L	F	A	Pts	Pos
42	14	13	15	63	61	41	11th

FA Cup

Rnd 3	Middlesbrough	(h)	3-1
Rnd 4	Brentford	(h)	0-0
Replay	Brentford	(a)	2-1
Rnd 5	Rotherham	(a)	3-1
Rnd 6	Everton	(h)	0-1

Brentford's legendary centre-forward Tommy Lawton
(number 9) can only watch as Villa clear yet another Bees
attack in the goalless FA Cup tie at Villa Park.

Villa fail to connect and Brentford live again — only to
lose the replay in London.

1953-4

We have already said that disastrous starts were part of the Villa trade mark during the early 1950s; boardroom upheavals also seem to trace a thread through the club's history and at the start of the 1953-4 season, Villa lost manager George Martin following a series of rumours amongst the shareholders of the club. In September 1953, Villa appointed a successor to Martin and their choice was received with unanimous approval. The club went to Notts County and prised their former star Eric Houghton back to Villa Park. Houghton had always been a firm favourite at Villa and he had done a good enough job at Meadow Lane to win the confidence of players, supporters and directors alike when he returned to Aston.

Houghton was soon busy installing new faces at the club. He was responsible for the signing of a nineteen-year-old Irishman called Peter McParland.

McParland was to win his place on Villa's left-wing and play a prominent part in winning the FA Cup in 1957, although the incident surrounding his challenge on Ray Wood was one of the less savoury facets of the game. Nevertheless, the youngster from Belfast was one of the most exciting players to watch in the entire Football League. Another of Houghton's signings was Bill Baxter from Wolverhampton Wanderers and although he never scaled the heights that McParland did, he was another useful addition to the Villa Park playing staff.

Alas, the 1953-4 season was a poor one as far as Villa were concerned. With Wolverhampton Wanderers winning the First Division

Villa's former player Eric Houghton returned to the club as manager in September 1953.

Championship and West Bromwich Albion taking the FA Cup at Wembley against Preston North End, Villa were pushed out of the Black Country's moment of soccer glory and they had to content themselves with thirteenth place in the table, having just failed to average a point a game from their fortytwo League matches.

Villa's one moment of real glory came in April 1954 when West Bromwich Albion came to Villa Park looking for two points which would keep them in the race for the First Division title and therefore, for the coveted League and Cup double last performed by Villa themselves during the last century. On the day there was no doubting who were the better side as Villa not only prevented their close rivals from taking any points from Villa Park, but did it to the convincing tune of 6–1. Villa's young attack scored seventy goals this season (there were four players — McParland, K. O. Roberts, Joe Tyrrell, and Derek Pace, all under twenty-two years of age when Villa scored that big win over West Brom) and Thompson led the scoring with twenty-one goals, followed by John Dixon and Dave Walshe. Ken Jones was now back in the Villa goal and the defence still featured Harry Parkes who played another great season at full-back with Peter Aldis alongside him for much of the time. Villa's rearguard conceded sixty-eight goals and there were two big defeats away from home — 6–1 at Liverpool and 4–0 at Huddersfield.

In the FA Cup, Villa went to Highbury for the third round but lost 5–1 to the Gunners who were in rampant form. The result capped a mediocre season for Villa fans and as soon as the cup was out of the way they went along to Villa Park knowing that their side had nothing to play for except a mid-table position. But Eric Houghton was preparing his plans for the future and, given the amount of time he had at his disposal in his first season as Villa team boss, he had done as well as anyone could expect.

First Division results 1953-4

	H	A
Arsenal	2–1	1–1
Blackpool	2–1	2–3
Bolton	2–2	0–3
Burnley	5–1	2–3
Cardiff	1–2	1–2
Charlton	2–1	1–1
Chelsea	2–2	2–1
Huddersfield	2–2	0–4
Liverpool	2–1	1–6
Manchester City	3–0	1–0
Manchester United	2–2	0–1
Middlesbrough	5–3	1–2
Newcastle	1–2	1–0
Portsmouth	1–1	1–2
Preston	1–0	1–1
Sheffield United	4–0	1–2
Sheffield Wed	2–1	1–3
Sunderland	3–1	0–2
Tottenham	1–2	0–1
West Brom	6–1	1–1
Wolves	1–2	2–1

Final League Record

P	W	D	L	F	A	Pts	Pos
42	16	9	17	70	68	41	13th

FA Cup

Rnd 3	Arsenal	(a)	1–5

Peter McParland made a great impression in his first season at Villa Park — and also scored twice in a dream debut for Northern Ireland in 1953-4.

1954-5

Forget the bad starts of previous Villa campaigns! This season was marked by one of the most sensational finishes to any Aston Villa season since the club was formed in 1874. In their last fifteen matches Villa won twenty-three points — including eleven clear-cut victories — and lifted themselves up the table into sixth position and only five points behind the surprise champions, Chelsea. It was championship form and if Villa had started their amazing run-in just four matches earlier, then they would probably have been the First Division's new title-holders.

Yet if Villa had lifted the Championship they would have been even bigger pretenders than the Stamford Bridge club. Villa had no real style and their magnificent late burst was as much due to endeavour and the run of the ball, as to outright skill. Nevertheless, they finished the season with a defensive record of only forty-seven goals against, which was their best for some years, although Sheffield Wednesday and Charlton each managed to score six goals against Villa away from Villa Park and Newcastle and Leicester (at Villa Park) hit them for five.

But the darkest parts of the season involved the departure of two fine players in Danny Blanchflower and Tommy Thompson, although Thompson's transfer did not take place until the close season when he joined Preston North End for £25,000. His going was a great loss to Villa but once he had seen Blanchflower seek new pastures, there was no holding the Scot. Blanchflower had asked for a move before the New Year, feeling that Villa were not going in the same direction that he would have wished for himself. The board debated and at last decided that there was no point in keeping an unhappy player on the books. As soon as he went on sale, Blanchflower was the target of several clubs but chiefly the north London rivals Spurs and Arsenal. Arsenal hung back a little and wanted Villa to drop the asking price of £30,000; Spurs had no such reservations and readily agreed to part with the cash. So Blanchflower became a Spurs player and Arsenal (and Villa) lived to regret the day.

Aston Villa's playing staff at the start of 1954-55. Before the season was out, Danny Blanchflower (back row, third from left) would be on his way to Spurs.

There had been backroom changes, too, as Villa brought back Jimmy Hogan to help out with the coaching. Hogan was now well past the age when most soccer coaches retire but he still had enough knowledge and skill in imparting it to make him a valuable addition to the staff where he helped the younger players with his immense fund of knowledge. In March 1955, Villa's chairman Mr F. H. Normansell died and his place was taken by the former Villa player Chris Buckley. Changing faces in the dressing room also brought Vic Crowe from local soccer, Roy Chapman, another junior who found the odd first team spot, and Tommy Southren who was signed from West Ham United on Christmas Eve 1954 for £12,000. Ex-Wolves full-back Roy Pritchard signed that winter but veterans Frank Moss and Harry Parkes retired from the game to end a Villa era.

In the FA Cup of 1954-5 Villa played seven matches but got only as far as the fourth round. After drawing 2–2 with Brighton at the Goldstone Ground they beat the Seasiders 4–2 at Villa Park in the third round replay. There followed no less than *five* games with Doncaster Rovers before Rovers finally won the fourth replay 3–1 at the Hawthorns. The sides had played 540 minutes of football before they eventually resolved the matter. Villa would have earned an away draw with Birmingham City had they won. As it was, Doncaster went to St Andrew's and lost 2–1.

First Division results 1954-5

	H	A
Arsenal	2–1	0–2
Blackpool	3–1	1–0
Bolton	3–0	3–3
Burnley	3–1	0–2
Cardiff	0–2	1–0
Charlton	1–2	1–6
Chelsea	3–2	0–4
Everton	0–2	1–0
Huddersfield	0–0	2–1
Leicester	2–5	2–4
Manchester City	2–0	4–2
Manchester United	2–1	1–0
Newcastle	1–2	3–5
Portsmouth	1–0	2–2
Preston	1–3	3–0
Sheffield Utd	3–1	3–1
Sheffield Wed	0–0	3–6
Sunderland	2–2	0–0
Tottenham	2–4	1–1
West Brom	3–0	3–2
Wolves	4–2	0–1

Final League Record

P	W	D	L	F	A	Pts	Pos
42	20	7	15	72	73	47	6th

FA Cup

Rnd 3	Brighton	(a)	2–2
Replay	Brighton	(h)	4–2
Rnd 4	Doncaster	(a)	0–0
Replay	Doncaster	(h)	2–2
Replay	Doncaster	(n)	1–1
Replay	Doncaster	(n)	0–0
Replay	Doncaster	(n)	1–3

Harry Parkes (left) and Frank Moss (right) retired during the season to bring to an end a great Villa era.

1955-6

There were to be no sensational doings towards the end of this season and it ended with Aston Villa missing relegation by the narrowest of margins. Things got from bad to worse each week and every Saturday plunged Villa Park further into the gloomy realisation that Second Division football was just around the corner. One of the more surprising aspects of this fall from grace was that Villa had dipped into their coffers and bought five expensive players in a bid to fight their way back up the First Division table. Some were successful signings; some were most definitely not.

Dave Hickson — the man who had knocked Villa out of the cup a few seasons earlier — came from Everton but within a short space of time he was moving on to Huddersfield Town, having failed quite dramatically to make an impact at Villa Park. Sheffield Wednesday's Jackie Sewell was signed in December 1955. Sewell was the man for whom Wednesday had paid Notts County the then record fee of £34,500 in 1951. In February 1956 Villa signed Jimmy Dugdale, the West Bromwich Albion centrehalf, together with Leslie Smith from Wolves; a month later, Smith's Wolves teammate, goalkeeper Nigel Sims was also on his way to Villa Park. A sixth new player came to the club when Millwall's young wing-half Pat Saward was signed from the London club. Dugdale had already won an FA Cup-winners medal with West Brom in 1954 and Smith was a Wolves regular, while Sims was to develop into one of the finest goalkeepers ever to wear a Villa jersey. A native of the Burton area, Sims had to understudy the great Bert Williams at Wolves and he grabbed his Villa opportunity with two safe hands; together with Saward, Houghton's latest signing would form the nucleus of the team which would win the FA Cup the following season.

In the First Division of 1955-6, however, Villa had a job to survive and it was only due to a spell of eleven games towards the end of the season in which they picked up fifteen points. Even then, they had to wait till the last day of the season before scraping home. When the last day came Villa had won only ten matches all season and were in twenty-first place. Sheffield United were already doomed and the final Second Division place rested between Villa and Huddersfield Town who were two points better off than the Claret and Blues. Villa faced their old Black Country rivals West Bromwich Albion at Villa Park in a game they had to win and win by a wide margin in order to survive. Earlier in the season West Brom had won 1-0 when the sides clashed in the League match at the Hawthorns and Villa fans were not at all

certain that their side would pull off a miracle. In fact, Villa won by the margin of three goals to nil, which was just good enough to save them and Huddersfield went down with a goal average just 0.2 worse than that of Villa.

In the FA Cup, Villa had struggled to dispose of Hull City after the Tigers had earned a 1-1 draw at Villa Park. Villa won the replay at Boothferry Park 2-1 but in the fourth round their old cup adversaries Arsenal trounced them 4-1 at Highbury and put another blot on the Villa season. Villa Park fans had little to which to look forward in the summer of 1956 — yet if only they could have seen into the immediate future, their hearts would have been lifted. Villa were going to Wembley again and they would take the FA Cup once more — for the first time in the lives of many supporters.

Dave Hickson was signed for a big fee from Everton in the autumn of 1955 but he never solved Villa's scoring problems and was soon on his way to Huddersfield.

Villa training 1950s style — a far cry from the sophisticated methods of the 1980s.

First Division results 1955-6

	H	A
Arsenal	1-1	0-1
Birmingham	0-0	2-2
Blackpool	1-1	0-6
Bolton	0-2	0-1
Burnley	2-0	0-2
Cardiff	2-0	0-1
Charlton	1-1	1-3
Chelsea	1-4	0-0
Everton	2-0	1-2
Huddersfield	3-0	1-1
Luton	1-0	1-2
Manchester City	0-3	2-2
Manchester Utd	4-4	0-1
Newcastle	3-0	3-2
Portsmouth	1-3	2-2
Preston	3-2	1-0
Sheffield Utd	3-2	2-2
Sunderland	1-4	1-5
Tottenham	0-2	3-4
West Brom	3-0	0-1
Wolves	0-0	0-0

Final League Record

P	W	D	L	F	A	Pts	Pos
42	'11	13	18	52	69	35	20th

FA Cup

Rnd 3	Hull City	(h)	1-1
Replay	Hull City	(a)	2-1
Rnd 4	Arsenal	(a)	1-4

1956-7

Aston Villa achieved two things in 1956-7; they won the FA Cup and, perhaps more importantly, they pulled themselves up the First Division table to finish in tenth place. And while in no way wishing to diminish the FA Cup win which was all-important to Villa Park fans, one ventures to suggest that First Division survival was more significant, although that would only be temporary.

But it is the cup for which the season will be remembered. They began their run in January and a visit to Luton Town's Kenilworth Road where the Hatters held Villa to a 2–2 draw. In the replay some 30,000 fans saw Leslie Smith cross for Johnny Dixon to head Villa in front; and then the same two players exchange passes before Dixon scored his second and put Villa through 2–0. In the fourth round Villa made the long journey to the north-east and Middlesbrough's Ayrsome Park. Clough and Harris gave Boro a 2–1 half-time lead, Smith having scored for Villa. Then Pace equalised and Dixon scored the winner when Middlesbrough's goalkeeper Peter Taylor was late in moving for the Villa player's shot.

Bristol City of the Second Division were Villa's fifth round opponents and they went down 2–1 at Villa Park. 60,000 fans saw Pace put Villa in front, John Atyeo equalise, and then Jackie Sewell score the winner with a fantastic goal of cool individual skill. Villa's jubilation was tempered when they learned that they had to travel to their bogey ground — Burnley's Turf Moor. It looked as though Villa's

run of bad results at Turf Moor would continue when Peter Aldis put through his own goal, but Peter McParland managed an equaliser and the clubs withdrew for a replay at Villa Park, where Dixon and McParland helped them to a 2–0 win. 45,000 fans roared Villa into the semi-final and a game with West Bromwich Albion.

The FA chose Wolves' Molineux for the semifinal — Birmingham were playing Manchester United at Hillsborough in the other semi-final —and on 23 March 1957 Villa's cup run looked to be over as West Brom led with just five minutes to play. But just as McParland scored Villa's first equaliser, so the Irishman bagged another and earned Villa yet another replay. 55,000 fans saw the first game at Wolves and 58,000 were at St Andrew's for the second match. When Albion's Ronnie Allen was injured with less than twenty minutes gone, Villa took command and in the thirty-eighth minute Billy Myerscough headed the only goal of the game. Although Albion hit the post and came near on other occasions, Villa hung on to go back to Wembley for the first time since before the war. They met

Aston Villa with the 1957 FA Cup. Back row, left to right: Peter Aldis, Stan Lynn, Nigel Simms, Stan Crowther, Peter McParland. Middle row: Eric Houghton (manager), Jackie Sewell, Billy Mysercough, Johnny Dixon, Leslie Smith, Bill Moore (trainer). Front row: Jimmy Dugdale, Pat Saward.

Manchester United, earlier on the road to a treble of FA Cup, First Division title and European Cup, although by cup final day they had been knocked out of Europe, but had won the League Championship.

In the sixth minute of the final, McParland clashed with United goalkeeper Ray Wood who was forced to go off with a fractured cheekbone. The incident would not have gone unpunished today, but in 1957 it was permissible. With centre-half Jackie Blanchflower in goal and with no substitute to call on, United did well but they were already beaten. Two goals within five minutes of each other in the second half — both scored by McParland — finished United off and although Tommy Taylor pulled back a goal, and although a groggy Wood eventually returned to goal, it was all over. The shame was that Villa's finest hour for years had been marred by the incident. But Villa *were* FA Cup holders.

The tragic incident in the 1957 FA Cup final when Ray Wood and Peter McParland collided.

First Division results 1956-7

	H	A
Arsenal	0–0	1–2
Birmingham	3–1	2–1
Blackpool	3–2	0–0
Bolton	0–0	0–0
Burnley	1–0	1–2
Cardiff	4–1	0–1
Charlton	3–1	2–0
Chelsea	1–1	1–1
Everton	5–1	4–0
Leeds	1–1	0–1
Luton	1–3	0–0
Manchester City	2–2	1–1
Manchester Utd	1–3	1–1
Newcastle	2–1	2–1
Portsmouth	2–2	1–5
Preston	2–0	3–3
Sheffield Wed	5–0	1–2
Sunderland	2–2	0–1
Tottenham	2–4	0–3
West Brom	0–0	0–2
Wolves	4–0	0–3

Final League Record

P	W	D	L	F	A	Pts	Pos
42	14	15	13	65	55	43	10th

FA Cup

Rnd 3	Luton Town	(a)	2–2
Replay	Luton Town	(h)	2–0
Rnd 4	Middlesbrough	(a)	3–2
Rnd 5	Bristol City	(h)	2–1
Rnd 6	Burnley	(a)	1–1
Replay	Burnley	(h)	2–0
Semi-final	West Brom	(n)	2–2
Replay	West Brom	(n)	1–0
Final	Manchester United (Wembley)		2–1

Villa skipper Johnny Dixon with the Cup.

1957-8

Manchester United fans did not have to wait long for their revenge. As League Champions, United met cup holders Villa in the FA Charity Shield at the beginning of the 1957-8 season and rubbed home their point by winning 4–0. It was the sign for which Villa should have been searching. Bad teams occasionally win the cup and Villa were at the very best, a mediocre side, despite those famous names. Yet they thought that the FA Cup win was a sure-fire sign that they would go on to greater things. They did not. Although it took them three games to do it, Stoke City knocked the cup holders out at the very first hurdle. City were then in the Second Division but they twice held Villa to a draw (1–1 at Villa Park and 3–3 at the Victoria Ground) before winning 2–0 in the second replay at Wolverhampton. Former Wolves player Dennis Wilshaw played a big part in his new club's win on his former club's ground.

But by the time Villa were knocked out of the cup, it was already obvious that the team needed major changes. In the end they were lucky to maintain fourteenth position in the First Division and the defence had let in the rather ominous total of eighty-six goals while nineteen matches were lost, including six-goal defeats at Leicester and Tottenham. Complacency was the name of the game at Villa Park. Throughout the season there were team changes and players coming and going from Villa Park. Pat Saward lost form and consequently his place in the side and Stan Crowther moved to Manchester United after they were stricken by the Munich aircrash. Crowther went on to play in his second successive FA Cup final and thus made a little piece of cup history by being the only player ever to have played in the competition for two clubs in the same season after the FA waived the qualification rules to help United out.

Derek Pace had already gone to Sheffield United and Billy Myerscough was also sadly out of form; the one bright spot was Johnny Dixon who reverted to wing-half in place of Crowther and played exceptionally well, although his switch meant that Villa were now short of his flair in the attack. Eventually, Villa went into the transfer market and signed Gerry Hitchens from Cardiff City. Hitchens was doing his National Service but was in fact a Cannock Chase lad and had made his name in the Southern League. Villa paid £22,500 for the player who had already won representative honours with England under-23's, the FA team and the powerful British Army side.

Even with Nigel Sims performing well in goal behind a defence of Stan Lynn and Peter Aldis at full-back and Jimmy Dugdale at centre-half, Villa's plight was obvious, though not perhaps to many actually at the club. It was certain that a general shake-up of the Villa Park structure was needed before they could come bouncing back in the best traditions of the club. It would, however, be some time before that shake-up was implemented — by which time Villa would be in the Second Division.

Villa Park's floodlights in the 1950s.

First Division results 1957-8

	H	A
Arsenal	3-0	0-4
Birmingham	0-2	1-3
Blackpool	1-1	1-1
Bolton	4-0	0-4
Burnley	3-0	0-3
Chelsea	1-3	2-4
Everton	0-1	2-1
Leeds	2-0	0-4
Leicester	5-1	1-6
Luton	2-0	0-3
Manchester City	1-2	2-1
Manchester Utd	3-2	1-4
Newcastle	4-3	4-2
Nottm Forest	1-1	1-4
Portsmouth	2-1	0-1
Preston	2-2	1-1
Sheffield Wed	2-0	5-2
Sunderland	5-2	1-1
Tottenham	1-1	2-6
West Brom	2-1	2-3
Wolves	2-3	1-2

Final League Record

P	W	D	L	F	A	Pts	Pos
42	16	7	19	73	86	39	14th

FA Cup

Rnd 3	Stoke City	(a)	1-1
Replay	Stoke City	(h)	3-3
Replay	Stoke City	(n)	0-2

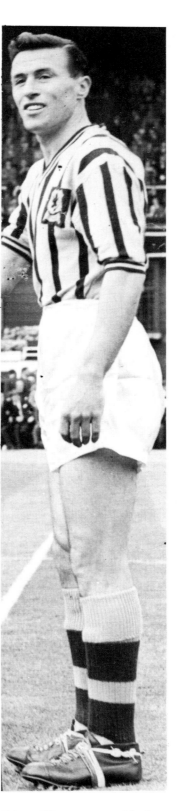

Johnny Dixon was moved back to wing-half in 1957-58 and was an immediate success.

1958-9

A black season for Aston Villa. In April 1959, Villa were relegated to the Second Division for only the second time in their long history. It was a doubly bitter pill for Villa fans to swallow since this same season saw Villa reach a record sixteenth FA Cup semi-final where a 1–0 defeat at the hands of Nottingham Forest saved them from the bizarre distinction of becoming the only club ever to have played at Wembley in an FA Cup final *and* been relegated in one and the same season.

There was another off-the-field row at the start of the season when — against the background of a team in bottom place in the First Division after five successive defeats — Villa's Shareholders Association tried to unseat two directors in favour of its own men. The bid failed and the directors, Joe Broughton and Bruce Normansell, retained their place on the Villa board.

Villa began their season with a 1–1 draw against Birmingham City at Villa Park and on the Monday following this opener, Portsmouth also visited Villa Park and lost 3–2. With three points from their first two matches, Villa could be forgiven for thinking that things were ticking over nicely. But there was that complacency again. The second Saturday of the season saw Villa go to Upton Park to meet newly-promoted West Ham United. The Hammers ran rings round Villa and won 7–2. The writing was on the wall.

Then Portsmouth won 5–2 against Villa at Fratton Park and Nottingham Forest came to Villa Park and beat the Claret and Blues 3–2; Wolves beat Villa quite convincingly in a midweek game and then Villa won their first point in a month when they managed to draw 1–1 with Blackpool, who lost centre-forward Dave Charnley, injured during the match. Wins over Blackburn and Newcastle gave Villa hope but then West Brom won 4–1 at Villa Park and to compound the problems, McParland put in for a transfer. Although he managed to change McParland's mind, Houghton was on the brink of resignation and his last signing was Ron Wylie from Notts County. The little Scottish forward came to Villa Park; and Houghton left, following a bleak November which had seen Villa scrape only five points out of a possible sixteen.

On Christmas Eve 1958, Villa were bottom of the First Division, having played twenty-three games for just seventeen points. At that point the club announced that they had appointed Joe Mercer as their manager in succession to Eric Houghton. Mercer, the former captain of Everton, Arsenal and England, came from Sheffield United where he had been team boss. Over Christmas, Mercer saw the magnitude of his task. Manchester United won 2–1 at Old Trafford and 2–0 at Villa Park and then West Ham won 2–1, also at Villa Park. Mercer's first signing was Doug Winton, the Burnley full-back who had played in Scotland's 'B' team, but he came too late to help Villa.

Nigel Sims — Villa's greatest goalkeeper since Sam Hardy.

Aston Villa 1958-9. Ron Wylie (front row, second from left) joined Villa from Notts County. He was Eric Houghton's last signing before the Villa manager gave way to Joe Mercer.

Although a few reasonable results gave Villa a little hope, the Easter programme put paid to them. On Good Friday, they lost 3–2 at White Hart Lane; on Easter Saturday, they lost 2–1 at Everton; and on Easter Monday, Spurs took a point in a 1–1 draw. When Leicester won 2–1 at Villa Park on 4 April, Villa knew they were doomed. When the last day of the season arrived, Villa had to beat West Brom while Manchester City had to lose to Leicester at Maine Road. City beat Leicester 3–1 at Maine Road, but even then, Villa were winning 1–0 with two minutes to go and they would have stayed up had not Ronnie Allen scored a last-gasp equaliser. They were relegated.

First Division results 1958-9

	H	A
Arsenal	1–2	2–1
Birmingham	1–1	1–4
Blackburn	1–0	3–2
Blackpool	1–1	1–2
Bolton	2–1	3–1
Burnley	0–0	1–3
Chelsea	3–1	1–2
Everton	2–4	1–2
Leeds	2–1	0–0
Leicester	1–2	3–6
Luton	3–1	1–2
Manchester City	1–1	0–0
Manchester Utd	0–2	1–2
Newcastle	2–1	0–1
Nottm Forest	2–3	0–2
Portsmouth	3–2	2–5
Preston	2–0	2–4
Tottenham	1–1	2–3
West Brom	1–4	1–1
West Ham	1–2	2–7
Wolves	1–3	0–4

Final League Record

P	W	D	L	F	A	Pts	Pos
42	11	8	23	58	87	30	21st

FA Cup

Rnd 3	Rotherham Utd	(h)	2–1
Rnd 4	Chelsea	(a)	2–1
Rnd 5	Everton	(a)	4–1
Rnd 6	Burnley	(h)	0–0
Replay	Burnley	(a)	2–0
Semi-final	Nottm Forest	(n)	0–1

1959-60

Aston Villa bounced straight back. At the first attempt Villa stormed away with the Second Division Championship, winning twenty-five of their matches and losing only eight, as well as reaching the semi-finals of the FA Cup before losing to Wolves in a close and thrilling cup-tie. Villa lost only one game at home and their defensive record of forty-three goals was not bettered by any club in the Football League. In addition, the presence of Aston Villa on some of the smaller grounds in the League proved to be of immense value to the home clubs and Lincoln, Rotherham and Scunthorpe each enjoyed a new attendance record when Villa were the visitors.

Villa began their Second Division programme with a 2–1 win at Brighton where Sewell grabbed the winner near the end of the match in a not-too-impressive Villa performance. In midweek Villa lost 1–0 at Roker Park but that was to be their last defeat for seventeen matches. By the time Liverpool won 2–1 at Anfield on 7 November, Villa were heading for the title. One week later, Villa confirmed they were too good for the Second Division with a staggering 11–1 win over Charlton Athletic at Villa Park. Gerry Hitchens scored five of the first six goals against a Charlton side which, it must be said, lost goalkeeper Duff with an arm injury, although by then Villa were already 6–1 ahead. McParland (2), Thomson (2), Wylie and MacEwan completed the rout.

Villa followed up this sensational win with 5–0 victories over Bristol City and Scunthorpe United and from then on there never looked to be any other Second Division winners but Villa, although Plymouth spoiled the end-of-season party when they inflicted Villa's heaviest defeat of the season (3–0 at Home Park) on the very last day of the season, by which time Villa were already assured of the title.

The FA Cup also provided Villa Park fans with some exciting moments in 1959-60. In the third round Villa beat Leeds United 2–1 at home. Although Leeds took the lead, Villa soon equalised through McParland and then Wylie scored the winner in front of a crowd of 40,000. In the fourth round, Villa travelled to Stamford Bridge and 66,000 fans saw the Midlanders win 2–1 with the goals coming from McParland and Thomson. Villa had also won at Stamford Bridge at the same stage of the cup exactly twelve months earlier. At Port Vale's ground in the fifth round, 49,000 somehow jammed themselves in to see the Potters give Villa quite a game. Vale scored first from a penalty and although Hitchens equalised early in the second half, Villa had to wait until six minutes from time before McEwan

crossed and Thomson headed the winner. In the quarter-finals Villa were drawn at home to Preston North End. Nearly 70,000 fans saw Tom Finney play his last big game at Villa Park and Hitchens gave Villa the lead after fifteen minutes. Near the end McParland made it 2–0 and Villa were into yet another semi-final.

They met Wolverhampton Wanderers at the Hawthorns where 55,000 managed to fit into a stadium for a game which could have attracted twice as many fans from the Black Country. In the thirty-first minute, Wolves scored the only goal of the game when Sims could not hold a fierce Murray drive and Deeley followed up to poke the ball home. Both sides had chances after that and near the end, Wolves goalkeeper Malcolm Finlayson did well to save what would have been Villa's equaliser. Wolves were the better side, but all that really mattered was that Villa were on target for First Division soccer once again.

Jimmy McEwan signed from Raith Rovers and had a blinder in the FA Cup tie against Chelsea.

Sports Argus

CITY FINAL

No. 2,874   Price 3d.   EVENING DESPATCH   Birmingham, Saturday, November 14, 1959

Walsall ten's Cup win : Coventry replay : Blues man ordered off (P.8) and...

VILLA 11, HITCHENS 5

VERDICT *by Dick Knight*

What Price this Villa attack now!

Aston Villa 11, Charlton 1

GERRY HITCHENS slammed his critics today in the best possible way—with five golden goals in this deep humiliation of Charlton.

I don't know what Joe Mercer had to say to his men this week over the recent scarcity of goals. I do know he has been worried about this — and Gerry has been on the verge of being dropped.

Justification for Hitchens and for Mercer's "unchanged" policy flowed from this runaway start. There's no room for Ken Price in this forward line at the moment. Charlton lost goalkeeper Willy Duff in the 40th minute, but Villa were 6—1 by then and the thrashing was well under way.

VILLA WERE RUTHLESS

By then Hitchens had done the damage with his own hand. Villa were ruthless. They were ahead in the second minute, surrendered that lead in the 22nd, but thereafter they went surging forward, slicing open the Charlton defence and romping in to bits as so much confetti.

VILLA WERE FAST, DIRECT AND FULL OF RUN. I liked best the way the ball came freely from defence and the way the whole of the forward line moved briskly forward, finding the open spaces. As for their finishing, the score line answers that.

These were Hitchens' first goals for a month and Bobby Thomson weighed in with a couple, his first since mid-September.

Bob Wylie managed one, too, but the clever Scotsman's value stood out, apart in the mid-field schemer with forward passes that would have split any defence in the land.

But for one shaky moment when Charlton scored, Villa's defence was firm and that's fair among against a Charlton forward line that has plenty to offer.

A GREAT SHOW FROM VILLA—THEIR BEST WIN FOR YEARS.

Tightness of defence, quickness on the ball and a forward line in this sort of mood must give them a chance high at the top of the Second Division table, and when the F.A. Cup comes along...

GOAL CHART—Aston Villa: Hitchens (2 mins, 29, 40, 44, 67), Thomson (28, 65), Wylie (63), MacEwan (69), McParland (72, 86). Charlton: Edwards (22).

ESTIMATED ATTENDANCE 22,000.

★ *It's goal No. 1 coming up* ★

This was the start of the move that brought Villa's two-minute goal at Villa Park. As the Charlton keeper comes out and Bobby Thomson challenges, the scorer, Gerry Hitchens (second from left), moves in to seize his opportunity.

A GREAT TWO-GOAL RALLY FAILS TO SAVE ALBION

VERDICT by Alan Lake

Blackburn 3, W.B. Albion 2

ALBION are still hunting their first away victory. The men from The Hawthorns went down 3—2 at Blackburn, after a ten-minute spell of scoring which produced four goals.

Rovers first effort was a fluke goal, Ally MacLeod's shot being deflected by Maurice Setters, but there are few grumbles about that score.

Albion's defence frequently looked shaky, and Don Howe will have to do better than this when he faces Peter McParland on the international on Wednesday.

The England right-back never curbed the lively MacLeod, while Joe Kennedy, too, looked ill at ease against David Whelan, the left-back having his first outing at centre forward.

ROBSON 'THE BEST FORWARD'

Bobby Robson was frequently Albion's "best forward." Though they twice pulled back after being a goal down, this front line is not good enough.

Alec Jackson and Andy Aitken were rarely in the picture, and for long spells Derek Kevan was ploughing a lone push up front.

DANY BURNSIDE — reduced Albion's arrears.

How the Birmingham Sports Argus heralded Villa's 11–1 victory over Charlton on November 14th 1959 when Gerry Hitchens grabbed five of the goals.

Second Division results 1959-60

	H	A
Brighton	3-1	2-1
Bristol City	2-1	5-0
Bristol Rovers	4-1	1-1
Cardiff	2-0	0-1
Charlton	11-1	0-2
Derby	3-2	2-2
Huddersfield	4-0	1-0
Hull	1-1	1-0
Ipswich	3-1	1-2
Leyton Orient	1-0	0-0
Lincoln	1-1	0-0
Liverpool	4-4	1-2
Middlesbrough	1-0	1-0
Plymouth	2-0	0-3
Portsmouth	5-2	2-1
Rotherham	3-0	1-2
Scunthorpe	5-0	2-1
Sheffield Utd	1-3	1-1
Stoke	2-1	3-3
Sunderland	3-0	0-1
Swansea Town	1-0	3-1

Final League Record

P	W	D	L	F	A	Pts	Pos
42	25	9	8	89	43	59	1st

FA Cup

Rnd 3	Leeds United	(h)	2-1
Rnd 4	Chelsea	(a)	2-1
Rnd 5	Port Vale	(a)	2-1
Rnd 6	Preston	(h)	2-0
Semi-final	Wolves	(n)	0-1

43

1960-1

While Joe Mercer spent much of 1960-1 rebuilding the Villa side with youth — the season's only signing was in February when Wolves reserve goalkeeper Geoff Sidebottom came to Villa Park — the club's first season after promotion was a more than satisfactory one as they reached the surprisingly high place of ninth in the First Division, got as far as the fifth round of the FA Cup, and became the first side to win the newly-inaugurated Football League Cup. In fact, the season's only real blackspot came at its conclusion when Gerry Hitchens (who scored forty-one goals that season) was transferred to Inter Milan for £85,000.

Villa started the season by beating Chelsea 3–2 at Villa Park; but after West Ham beat them 5–2 at Upton Park and Blackpool won 5–3 at Bloomfield Road, Mercer made changes and out went Sims, Dugdale and Saward. Villa then won four of the next six games including a 3–1 victory over Manchester United at Villa Park, but then met Spurs at White Hart Lane. This was the Spurs side which was racing to the double, last achieved by Villa, and after storming into a 4–0 half-time lead, Tottenham finished 6–2 winners. When Leicester won 3–1 at Villa Park, Mercer rang the changes yet again. In matches against fellow Black Country sides Villa fared well, however. Fifty thousand saw them beat Birmingham 6–2 at Villa Park and West Brom were beaten 2–0 at the Hawthorns, although Albion snatched both points in the return game and Wolves did the double over Villa. Nevertheless, ninth place

was good and a placing that Villa fans would gladly have settled for at the start of the season. Hitchens goals left him just two behind the First Division's leading scorer, Jimmy Greaves of Spurs, and Vic Crowe, who had assumed the Villa captaincy, played a total of fifty-three matches in all competitions.

In the FA Cup, Villa were eventually knocked out by Tottenham as the Spurs drove on relentlessly to Wembley. In the third round of the competition Villa were drawn away to Bristol Rovers at Eastville where the Pirates held on to a 1–1 draw before being comprehensively thrashed 4–0 at Villa Park. The fourth round gave Villa an awkward tie against Peterborough United at London Road. Posh were the team of the moment. After dominating the Midland League for so long, they were storming away with the Fourth Division Championship (and in doing so, beating Villa's record number of goals in a season). Villa were lucky to leave Northamptonshire with a 1–1 draw and the replay drew 64,000 to Villa Park where home advantage saw Villa home 2–1 with Peter McParland scoring both goals, although Posh were again unlucky and caused Villa plenty of anxious moments.

And so to the fifth round and mighty Spurs at Villa Park. One week before the teams met in the cup, they had played a First Division game at Villa

Aston Villa's full playing staff at the start of 1960-1.

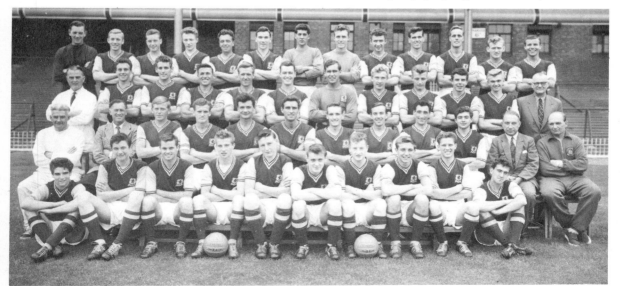

First Division results 1960-1

	H	A
Arsenal	2-2	1-2
Birmingham	6-2	1-1
Blackburn	2-2	1-4
Blackpool	2-2	3-5
Bolton	4-0	0-3
Burnley	2-0	1-1
Cardiff	2-1	1-1
Chelsea	3-2	4-2
Everton	3-2	2-1
Fulham	2-1	1-1
Leicester	1-3	1-3
Manchester City	5-1	1-4
Manchester Utd	3-1	1-1
Newcastle Utd	2-0	1-2
Nottm Forest	1-2	0-2
Preston	1-0	1-1
Sheffield Wed	4-1	2-1
Tottenham	1-2	2-6
West Brom	0-1	2-0
West Ham	2-1	2-5
Wolves	0-2	2-3

Final League Record

P	W	D	L	F	A	Pts		Pos
42	17	9	16	78	77	43		9th

FA Cup

Rnd 3	Bristol Rov	(a)	1-1
Replay	Bristol Rov	(h)	4-0
Rnd 4	Peterborough	(a)	1-1
Replay	Peterborough	(h)	2-1
Rnd 5	Tottenham	(h)	0-2

Football League Cup

Rnd 2	Huddersfield	(h)	4-1
Rnd 3	Preston	(a)	3-3
Replay	Preston	(h)	3-1
Rnd 4	Plymouth	(h)	3-3
Replay	Plymouth	(a)	0-0
Replay	Plymouth	(n)	5-3
Rnd 5	Wrexham	(h)	3-0
Semi-final (1st leg) Burnley		(a)	1-1
Semi-final (2nd leg) Burnley		(h)	2-2
Replay	Burnley	(n)	2-1
Final (1st leg) Rotherham		(a)	0-2
Final (2nd leg) Rotherham		(h)	3-0

Aston Villa won 3-2 on aggregate.

Park which Spurs won 2-1. Thus fortified by a morale-boosting win (if, indeed, Spurs needed their morale boosting), Tottenham duly won the cup-tie. A crowd of 65,474 saw Villa never get out of second gear. John Neal gave them the worst possible start by putting through his own goal and Cliff Jones added a second. Spurs then sat back, content to control the game without going berserk. Spurs returned to Villa Park for the semi-final when some 70,000 saw them beat Burnley.

Villa were not one of the First Division clubs which shunned the first Football League Cup competition. The result was that Villa took the trophy and although the final was held over until the following season, it is recorded here because Villa are held as the holders for 1960-1. Huddersfield, Preston, Plymouth and Wrexham were removed on the way to the semi-finals, although it took Villa two games to dispose of Preston and three to get rid of Plymouth. In the two-legged semi-final, neither Villa nor Burnley could resolve the tie and that too went to a replay before Villa won 2-1 at Old Trafford. At the start of the following season Villa lost 2-0 in the first-leg at Rotherham and then won 2-0 before 40,000 fans at Villa Park to level the aggregate. The game went into extra-time and in the nineteenth minute of the extra period, McParland scored a third goal to ensure that Villa's name was the first on the new cup.

Gerry Hitchens bursts through the West Brom defence in Villa's 2-0 win at the Hawthorns in November 1960.

1961-2

In July 1961, Joe Mercer signed big Derek Dougan from Blackburn Rovers. The Irish international was to become a big name in the players' union but at the start of this season Villa fans were only interested in the possibility of the big Irishman proving a worthy deputy for Gerry Hitchens who had gone off to seek his fortune in Italy. Unfortunately, Dougan was to miss much of the season after sustaining injuries in a car accident, but before he did Villa Park fans sensed that he was something special. Players who left the club before the start of the season included Jimmy Adam (to Stoke), Doug Winton (to Rochdale), and Mike Kenning and Terry Morrall (both to Shrewsbury). Young Villa players making their way into the first team included Harry Burrows, John Sleeuwenhoek, and Charlie Aitken. Sleeuwenhoek, through his Dutch father, was known as 'Johnny Tulip' and he had played with England schoolboys as a centre-half. Burrows had joined Villa straight from school in Lancashire and had made his debut in the forward line in 1958. Aitken was good enough to win a place in the Scotland under-23s this season.

After they had won the League Cup against Rotherham early in September, Villa lost the services of Dougan after he and Bobby Thomson were involved in a car crash. Dougan suffered head injuries which kept him out of the side until December, but Thomson was saved serious injury and, ironically, it was to him that Villa turned in seeking a replacement for their Irish star. Peter McParland was also drafted in at centre-forward where he gave his usual competitive performance.

Villa climbed further up the First Division to finish in seventh place and there were some memorable League games to recall. At Highbury, Villa and Arsenal were drawing 4–4 with the seconds ticking away in a thrilling match when Tommy Ewing, the diminutive winger who Villa had signed from Partick Thistle for £20,000, popped up to crack home a last-gasp equaliser; when Blackpool came to Villa Park they were hammered 5–0 with Peter McParland seemingly in at every kill; and over Easter, Villa scored thirteen goals in two games against Leicester and Nottingham Forest. On Easter Saturday, Leicester came to Villa Park and even the great Gordon Banks could not prevent them from going down 8–3 with Thomson scoring a great hat-trick. On Easter Monday, Harry Burrows scored the first goal against Forest at Villa Park before the game was two minutes old and Villa won 5–1. The one drawback to the League season was when Birmingham City, struggling manfully to avoid

relegation to the Second Division, won 3–1 at Villa Park.

Strangely, Villa were also involved in another match which decided the double hopes of another club. Burnley were going on to win the FA Cup and they also vied with Alf Ramsey's Ipswich for the First Division title. Ipswich needed to win their final home match, which was against Villa, and this they duly did to prevent Burnley from becoming the second successive team to win both major trophies.

Villa's hopes of retaining the Football League Cup were dashed as early as the third round. After beating West Ham at Upton Park, Villa lost to Ipswich at Villa Park. Villa fought through to the sixth round of the FA Cup, although they might well have gone out as early as the third round when third Division Crystal Palace ran them close at Villa Park. Palace twice took the lead and it was only a hopeful half-shot-half-centre which finally allowed Burrows to net the winning goal and send Villa through 4–3. After Huddersfield and Charlton, Villa faced Spurs and lost 2–0 as most people expected that they would. Perhaps the happiest man at Villa Park in 1961-2 was Harry Burrows who finished as leading scorer with twenty-one goals in all competitions.

Sims fails to stop Leicester equalising at Villa Park on April 21 1962. But Villa went on to win 8-3 — the second time in their history that they had beaten Leicester by that rare scoreline.

First Division results 1961-2

	H	A
Arsenal	3–1	5–4
Birmingham	1–3	2–0
Blackburn	1–0	2–4
Blackpool	5–0	2–1
Bolton	3–0	1–1
Burnley	0–2	0–3
Cardiff	2–2	0–1
Chelsea	3–1	0–1
Everton	1–1	0–2
Fulham	2–0	1–3
Ipswich	3–0	0–2
Leicester	8–3	2–0
Manchester City	2–1	0–1
Manchester Utd	1–1	0–2
Nottm Forest	5–1	0–2
Sheffield Utd	0–0	2–0
Sheffield Wed	1–0	0–3
Tottenham	0–0	0–1
West Brom	1–0	1–1
West Ham	2–4	0–2
Wolves	1–0	2–2

Final League Record

P	W	D	L	F	A	Pts	Pos
42	18	8	16	65	56	44	7th

FA Cup

Rnd 3	Crystal Palace	(h)	4–3
Rnd 4	Huddersfield	(h)	2–1
Rnd 5	Charlton	(h)	2–1
Rnd 6	Tottenham	(a)	0–2

Football League Cup

Rnd 1	Bradford C	(a)	4–3
Rnd 2	West Ham Utd	(a)	3–1
Rnd 3	Ipswich	(h)	2–3

1962-3

The 1962-3 season was disrupted by the blanket of snow and ice that held the country in its grip for over three months. The break in mid-season meant that Villa would never regain the splendid motion which had carried them to the beginning of December in such fine style. The result was that Villa fell down the First Division and finished in fifteenth place, although they also reached their second Football League Cup final — a feat which was tempered by the fact that they lost to Birmingham City in the two-legged final.

When the season opened in glorious sunshine, there was no sign of the dreadful winter to follow and Villa's young team came to Villa Park and scored a superb 3–1 win over West Ham United to give their fans great hope for the coming campaign. In midweek, Derek Dougan scored both the goals which sunk Spurs 2–1, also at Villa Park, and Villa followed this up by beating Manchester City 2–0 at Maine Road. Even when Spurs won 4–2 at White Hart Lane, Villa came back, drawing 1–1 with Blackpool and beating Arsenal 2–1 at Highbury. By the middle of November, Villa were seventh in the table and they continued their good run, signing Phil Woosnam from West Ham for £27,000. Bolton were beaten 5–0 just before Christmas and that proved to be the watershed in Villa's First Division programme.

Villa did not play a match between 19 January and 9 March and when they did begin to feel their way again, the form which had taken them to the fringes of the championship race escaped them. At one stage, after a string of defeats, Villa had stumbled down to eighteenth position and were in danger of making a relatively swift return to the Second Division. The final League match of the season was against Liverpool at Villa Park and Joe Mercer gave a first debut to a young player called George Graham. Graham scored a goal on his first appearance in senior football, Liverpool were beaten 2–0, and Villa were safe. It seems incredible that Graham was subsequently sold to Chelsea for £5,000. They were soon to part with Derek Dougan, too, and his transfer to Peterborough United in June for just £16,000 marked another black mark on the Villa end-of-term report. McParland went to Wolves for £30,000.

In the FA Cup of 1962-3, Villa again had to contend with the weather. They were drawn away to Bristol City in the third round and drew 1–1, before winning the replay 3–2 and then going down 1–0 at Old Trafford. United — like the four winners of the Cup immediately before them — had to beat Villa to take the trophy. It was the Football League Cup which brought Villa most hope of glory. They crushed Peterborough United 6–1 at Villa Park, beat

Charlie Aitken fails to block a shot by Blackburn Rovers. But the ball went wide and the sides drew 0-0 in January 1963.

Villa winger Ewing gets in a diving header — but Birmingham goalkeeper Schofield gathers it cleanly at Villa Park in March 1963. Schofield was less lucky overall as Villa steamed home 4-0.

First Division results 1962-3

	H	A
Arsenal	3-1	2-1
Birmingham	4-0	2-3
Blackburn	0-0	1-4
Blackpool	1-1	0-4
Bolton	5-0	1-4
Burnley	2-1	1-3
Everton	0-2	1-1
Fulham	1-2	0-1
Ipswich	4-2	1-1
Leicester	3-1	3-3
Leyton Orient	1-0	2-0
Liverpool	2-0	0-4
Manchester City	3-1	2-0
Manchester Utd	1-2	2-2
Nottm Forest	0-2	1-3
Sheffield Utd	1-2	1-2
Sheffield Wed	0-2	0-0
Tottenham	2-1	2-4
West Brom	2-0	0-1
West Ham	3-1	1-1
Wolves	0-2	1-3

Final League Record

P	W	D	L	F	A	Pts	Pos
42	15	8	19	62	68	38	15th

FA Cup

Rnd 3	Bristol City	(a)	1-1
Replay	Bristol City	(h)	3-2
Rnd 4	Manchester United	(a)	0-1

Football League Cup

Rnd 2	Peterborough	(h)	6-1
Rnd 3	Stoke	(h)	3-1
Rnd 4	Preston	(h)	6-2
Rnd 5	Norwich	(h)	4-1
Semi-final (1st leg) Sunderland		(a)	3-1
Semi-final (2nd leg) Sunderland		(h)	0-0
Final (1st leg) Birmingham		(a)	1-3
Final (2nd leg) Birmingham		(h)	0-0

Aston Villa lost 3-1 on aggregate.

Stoke 3-1, and then hammered another six goals past Preston North End to reach the quarter-finals where they disposed of Norwich 4-1. In a two-legged semi-final Villa were assured of a final place when they won 3-1 at Sunderland, holding on to a 0-0 draw at Villa Park. They had only to travel across the city to St Andrew's for the first-leg of the final but the Blues won 3-1 and then held Villa 0-0 at Villa Park. It was a repeat in reverse of Villa's semi-final scoreline against Sunderland, and Birmingham fully deserved their win, for Villa never turned on the form which had got them to the final. In fact, Villa's season can be strictly divided into two halves — before the ice age and after. And the interceding lull cost them dearly.

1963-4

This was a black season for Aston Villa. They slumped to nineteenth place in the First Division, missed relegation by the skin of their teeth, and were knocked out of both the FA Cup and the Football League Cup in the earliest stages, with the FA Cup exit proving particularly humiliating at the hands of humble Aldershot.

In July 1963, Villa paid £23,000 for Notts County's giant centre-forward Tony Hateley. Twenty-two-year-old Hateley was born in Derby and had a fearsome reputation as a striker. He was, Villa felt, just the man to succeed Derek Dougan, the man who had never hit it off at Villa Park. The season was also the last at Villa Park for manager Joe Mercer whose illness led to him resigning from the job. By the time Villa had been bundled out of the FA Cup, Villa's fans were in no mood to tolerate any more unpleasant shocks and, as is often the case in football, the manager's head had to roll.

With considerable structural alterations giving Villa Park a new look, the side kicked off the season, hoping to emulate the previous season's run which had taken them to the First Division top-ten before winter struck. Hateley was joined in the Villa first team by several other new faces including Mick Wright who came into the defence. Hateley scored seventeen goals in the League and with Burrows weighing in with sixteen, the pair looked to have hit it off. But Villa had allowed Bobby Thomson to leave for Birmingham before the season was a couple of months old, even though he had found the net quite regularly, and Villa fans complained that their club was too fond of letting players go. They pointed to Dougan and to Derek Pace. Pace was a prime example because since leaving Villa Park he had been Sheffield United's leading scorer for six consecutive seasons. And when United won 1-0 at Villa Park that season, it was Pace who knocked home the winner to rub salt into Villa's wounds.

In the Football League Cup, Villa beat Barnsley and were rewarded with another home draw against West Ham United. This time, however, Villa were beaten 2-0 and shortly after the game, Mercer went into the transfer market and bought Shrewsbury Town's David Pountney for £20,000. Pountney was a useful signing. He was a powerfully-built wing-half who had made over 200 appearances for the Gay Meadow club. But it was an easy-looking third round FA Cup tie which altered the shape of things at Villa Park. In the first match — played on Villa's home ground — Aldershot, with luck and a brilliant goalkeeper, managed a goalless draw. When Villa went down to Hampshire for the replay they were beaten by the tiny Recreation Ground's cramped atmosphere and Aldershot won 2-1. It was a terrible fate to befall such a mighty cup-fighting club as Villa.

Villa v Ipswich, November 1963. Deakin has the ball in the Suffolk club's net but the goal is disallowed and the scoreline finished 0-0.

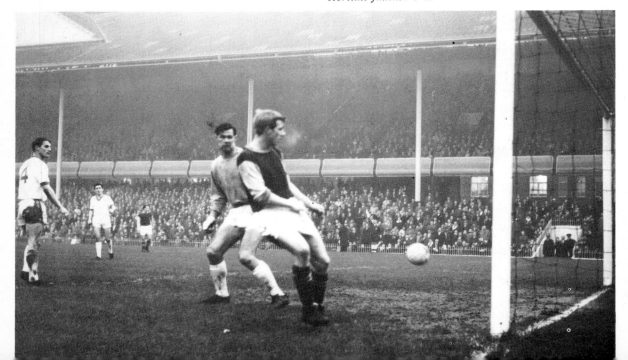

The result also saw the end of Joe Mercer as Villa's manager. He had been overworking and the additional burden of Villa's poor performances and strokes of ill-luck, like Phil Woosnam being taken ill, meant that his health gave way. One morning Mercer was polishing his car when he felt unwell. The doctor called it 'hypertension' and every football manager in the country knew just how Joe Mercer felt. It was left to his assistant, Dick Taylor, to bring Villa away from relegation. He managed it — but only just.

First Division results 1963-4

	H	A
Arsenal	2-1	0-3
Birmingham	0-3	3-3
Blackburn	1-2	0-2
Blackpool	3-1	4-0
Bolton	3-0	1-1
Burnley	2-0	0-2
Chelsea	2-0	0-1
Everton	0-1	2-4
Fulham	2-2	0-2
Ipswich	0-0	3-4
Leicester	1-3	0-0
Liverpool	2-2	2-5
Manchester United	4-0	0-1
Nottm Forest	3-0	1-0
Sheffield Utd	0-1	1-1
Sheffield Wed	2-2	0-1
Stoke	1-3	2-2
Tottenham	2-4	1-3
West Brom	1-0	3-4
West Ham	2-2	1-0
Wolves	2-2	3-3

Final League record

P	W	D	L	F	A	Pts	Pos
42	11	12	19	62	71	34	19th

FA Cup

Rnd 3	Aldershot	(h)	0-0
Replay	Aldershot	(a)	1-2

Football League Cup

Rnd 2	Barnsley	(h)	3-1
Rnd 3	West Ham	(h)	0-2

Dave Charnley of Blackpool outjumps John Sleeuwenhoek and heads towards Villa's goal in January 1964. Villa won the match 3-1 to ease their relegation worries.

1964-5

Dick Taylor was the official manager of Aston Villa as the club began the 1964-5 season. Taylor began his career as a player with Wolverhampton Wanderers before spending most of his playing days with Grimsby. He had served Scunthorpe United and Sheffield United (under Mercer) as trainer-coach before following his old boss to Villa Park where he had been six years.

The first game of this season gave Taylor little comfort as Villa lost 2–1 at home to Leeds United who had just been promoted to the First Division under their new manager, Don Revie. By the middle of September, Villa had lost four games out of the opening six and had conceded fifteen goals. During that spell they made their first signing under Taylor's regime when Arsenal's Scottish international winger Johnny MacLeod came to Villa Park for £30,000, which was a record for Villa at that time. Villa won their first match by beating Sunderland 2–1 at home but by the end of September they were bottom of the table, one point worse off than Wolves.

A 2–0 win over Sheffield Wednesday raised them to last-but-one position but after a surprise League Cup win at Leeds, Villa came back to earth with a resounding bump when they travelled to

A sunny start to a sunny afternoon as Phil Woosnam (not in picture) heads Villa into a third-minute lead over Leeds in August 1964. But the clouds soon came out for Villa who lost 2-1.

Manchester United's Old Trafford and were soundly thrashed 7–0. Dennis Law scored four goals, in direct contrast to the fortunes of Villa's Hateley who was carried off with an injury. Taylor continued to make signings. Barry Stobart, the former Wolves forward, returned to the Black Country from Manchester City for £30,000 and Villa also brought goalkeeper Colin Withers to Villa Park for £18,000. Other players to join Villa during this season were Willie Hamilton, the Hibs inside-forward; John Woodward from Stoke; and Tony Scott from West Ham. Out later went the veteran Jimmy MacEwan, given a free transfer to Walsall; Harry Burrows to Stoke City; Ron Wylie to Notts County; and Bill Atkins to Stockport. Villa spent the whole season in the bottom four of the First Division and at the end of it they were fortunate to maintain sixteenth place and missed relegation by six points. The defence had conceded eighty-two goals.

In the FA Cup, Villa started brightly with a 3–0 home third round win over Coventry. Phil Woosnam spurred Villa on before over 47,000, about half of them from Coventry. In the fourth round Villa beat Sheffield United 2–0 at Bramall Lane and that brought them into an eyeball to eyeball confrontation with Wolves at Villa Park. Hateley scored for Villa as the sides drew 1–1 and withdrew to fight again at Molineux. Over 52,000 fans had seen the first match and 48,000 crammed the Wolves ground for the replay which resulted in a goalless draw. The second replay was at the Hawthorns and

Leeds striker Storrie cannot get his head to this punched clearance from Sidebottom.

First Division results 1964-5

	H	A
Arsenal	3–1	1–3
Birmingham	3–0	1–0
Blackburn	0–4	1–5
Blackpool	3–2	1–3
Burnley	1–0	2–2
Chelsea	2–2	1–2
Everton	1–2	1–3
Fulham	2–0	1–1
Leeds	1–2	0–1
Leicester	1–0	1–1
Liverpool	0–1	1–5
Manchester United	2–1	0–7
Nottm Forest	2–1	2–4
Sheffield Utd	2–1	2–4
Sheffield Wed	2–0	1–3
Stoke	3–0	1–2
Sunderland	2–1	2–2
Tottenham	1–0	0–4
West Brom	0–1	1–3
West Ham	2–3	0–3
Wolves	3–2	1–0

Final League Record

P	W	D	L	F	A	Pts	Pos
42	16	5	21	57	82	37	16th

this time Villa fell as the hungry Wolves snapped at their heels relentlessly all evening to win 3–1.

Just as Villa had been the FA Cup side of their day, so they were gaining a reputation in the Football League Cup and in 1964-5 they went back to their third semi-final. Luton, Leeds, Reading and Bradford City (by a score of 7–1 with Hateley scoring four times) gave Villa a semi-final against Chelsea. The first leg was played at Villa Park and when Chelsea won 3–2, Villa knew that their task for the return at Stamford Bridge would be a hard one. They were right. They could only draw 1-1 and it was Chelsea who went through to the final while Villa were left to strive for First Division survival as best they could.

FA Cup

Rnd 3	Coventry	(h)	3–0
Rnd 4	Sheffield Utd	(a)	2–0
Rnd 5	Wolves	(h)	1–1
Replay	Wolves	(a)	0–0
Replay	Wolves	(n)	1–3

Football League Cup

Rnd 2	Luton	(a)	1–0
Rnd 3	Leeds	(a)	3–2
Rnd 4	Reading	(h)	3–1
Rnd 5	Bradford C	(h)	7–1
Semi-final (1st leg) Chelsea	(h)	2–3
Semi-final (2nd leg) Chelsea	(a)	1–1

Aston Villa lost 3–4 on aggregate.

1965-6

It is to the eternal credit of Dick Taylor that he contrived to keep Villa in the First Division during this period and although football fans will always cry for the blood of a manager when things are not going well, it is doubtful whether Villa fans realised the full traumas and tribulations that Taylor was enduring, particularly as his side was plagued for much of his reign with injuries and illness which often robbed him of his key players at the most crucial times.

In 1965-6 Villa managed to stay afloat and in fact pulled away from the relegation zone to the extent that when the season ended, they had climbed to sixteenth position. So, twice in consecutive seasons, Taylor had breathed enough life into Villa to give them a final placing some way from the relegated clubs. In the previous campaign, it had been Birmingham and Wolves who went down to complete a disastrous season for the Black Country;

this time Northampton and Blackburn were the unlucky pair. Villa's escape looked like this in the final table:

		P	W	D	L	F	A	Pts
16	Aston Villa	42	15	6	21	69	80	36
17	Sheff Wed	42	14	8	20	56	66	36
18	Nottm Forest	42	14	8	20	56	72	36
19	Sunderland	42	14	8	20	51	72	36
20	Fulham	42	14	7	21	67	85	35
21	Northampton	42	10	13	19	55	92	33
22	Blackburn	42	8	4	30	57	88	20

Whereas Villa had finished in the same position as the previous season, in 1964-5 they had missed the drop by seven points — in 1965-6 the gap had been a mere three, although in the previous season they had won only one more point. There were some shocking results this season. Relegated Northampton Town had beaten Villa twice — they won only ten games all season — and Manchester United had thrashed Villa 6-1 at Old Trafford, although Villa had themselves scored six goals against fellow relegation strugglers Fulham at Craven Cottage. In addition, Villa also managed five goals at White Hart Lane, only on that occasion Spurs also completed a nap hand and the result was a rare 5-5 draw. Villa had conceded eighty goals and it was obvious that unless some major surgery was carried out quickly, then they would not remain in the First Division for very much longer. Off the field, Villa's transfer dealings totted up to a debit of over £21,000, which was quite a lot of money then. To add to the problem, the dealings had probably resulted in Villa having a weaker side when they should have been building a stronger one.

In the FA Cup, Leicester City came to Villa Park in early January and won 2-1 to complete an unhappy post-Christmas period for Villa fans. Only the Football League Cup looked a likely source of glory and Villa managed two good wins in the second and third rounds. First they won an awkward tie at Swansea 3-2, then travelled to Roker Park and won 2-1,— always a feat on Wearside. In the fourth round Villa forced a 1-1 draw at Fulham before winning the Villa Park replay 2-0. There the cup run ended. In the fifth round, West Bromwich Albion took full advantage of their home advantage at the Hawthorns and won 3-1. For yet another season, Villa's only involvement as the programme was drawing to a close was to survive for another twelve months in the First Division. Soon, there would be no escape.

First Division results 1965-6

	H	A
Arsenal	3-0	3-3
Blackburn	3-1	2-0
Blackpool	3-0	1-0
Burnley	2-1	1-3
Chelsea	2-4	2-0
Everton	3-2	0-2
Fulham	2-5	6-3
Leeds	0-2	0-2
Leicester	2-2	1-2
Liverpool	0-3	1-3
Manchester Utd	1-1	1-6
Newcastle	4-2	0-1
Northampton	1-2	1-2
Nottm Forest	3-0	2-1
Sheffield Utd	0-2	0-1
Sheffield Wed	2-0	0-2
Stoke	0-1	0-2
Sunderland	3-1	0-2
Tottenham	3-2	5-5
West Brom	1-1	2-2
West Ham	1-2	2-4

Final League Record

P	W	D	L	F	A	Pts	Pos
42	15	6	21	69	80	36	16th

FA Cup

Rnd 3	Leicester	(h)	1-2

Football League Cup

Rnd 2	Swansea	(a)	3-2
Rnd 3	Sunderland	(a)	2-1
Rnd 4	Fulham	(a)	1-1
Replay	Fulham	(h)	2-0
Rnd 5	West Brom	(a)	1-3

Aston Villa's line-up 1965-66. Phil Woosnam (middle row, second from left) is now soccer supremo in the United States.

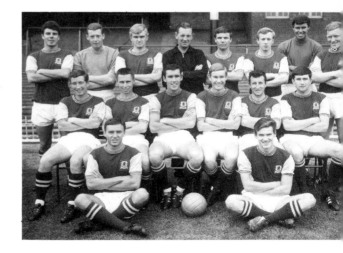

◄ *Big Tony Hateley out-soars the Fulham defence to head a Villa equaliser. But the Cottagers came back to win 5-2 in March 1966.*

1966-7

The season started with Villa losing two of their best-known players; it ended with the club at last bowing to the inevitable and going down to the Second Division. In many ways, Villa's relegation was almost a kindness because the club had battled so long against the drop with ever-failing resources. Of all the seasons which Dick Taylor had to endure, this was his worst, with several of his team again sidelined at critical times.

September saw the departure of Welsh international winger Phil Woosnam. Woosnam had been a familiar figure in the Villa Park set up, with his crew-cut hairstyle and speedy runs down the wing. He left England altogether and flew to the United States where he became involved — and still is — with the bid to establish soccer in America. Woosnam at first went to play for Atlanta but quickly rose to the top of the American soccer hierarchy. The following month saw Tony Hateley leave Villa Park. The big centre-forward was off on another ride on his multi-thousand pound merry-go-round which eventually took him to such clubs as far apart as Chelsea and Liverpool. This time it was to Stamford Bridge that Hateley was bound, having asked for a transfer one day and being sold for £100,000 the next. In some ways, that figure seemed more significant than the £1 million transfers of today. In 1966, we were still not used to inflation. Hateley had scored eighty-six goals in 148 first team appearances for Villa. It was a fine record.

The pre-Christmas period saw Villa go into the transfer market themselves and Dick Taylor pinned much of his hopes on Peter Broadbent, the Wolverhampton Wanderers veteran forward. Broadbent's best days were over but he did contribute something to a Villa side full of young and relatively inexperienced players. Just before Christmas, Villa beat Manchester United 2-1 at Villa Park and this gave the fans a little Yuletide cheer. But as New Year's Day dawned, the club faced 1967 in extreme difficulty with much less than a point a game from their partially completed programme.

In the FA Cup there was a little ray of hope when Villa beat Preston North End 1-0 at Deepdale; but in the fourth round they went to Anfield and lost 1-0. Earlier in the season West Brom had inflicted a crushing blow to Villa's morale by winning 6-1 at the Hawthorns in the second round of the Football League Cup.

With the cups out of the way there was only the League to concentrate on and Villa began to slide deeper and deeper into the mire of relegation. In early April, Fulham came to Villa Park with Johnny Haynes — the first £100 per week footballer in Britain — making his 500th League appearance for the Cottagers. At that time Villa stood in twenty-first place, level on points with West Brom. Blackpool were already beyond rescue. Fulham drew 1-1 and when Nottingham Forest beat Villa 3-0 at the City Ground, relegation looked certain. It was. Villa took only one point from the next four matches and in the last game of the season, Southampton finally hammered the last nail into Villa's already tightly-sealed coffin by winning 6-2 at The Dell. Villa were down again and this time their fans realised that they had no right to a permanent place in the top drawer of soccer. Aston Villa were, well and truly, a Second Division side.

First Division results 1966-7

	H	A
Arsenal	0-1	0-1
Blackpool	3-2	2-0
Burnley	0-1	2-4
Chelsea	2-6	1-3
Everton	2-4	1-3
Fulham	1-1	1-5
Leeds	3-0	2-0
Leicester	0-1	0-5
Liverpool	2-3	0-1
Manchester City	3-0	1-1
Manchester United	2-1	1-3
Newcastle	1-1	3-0
Nottm Forest	1-1	0-3
Sheffield Utd	0-0	3-3
Sheffield Wed	0-1	0-2
Southampton	0-1	2-6
Stoke	2-1	1-6
Sunderland	2-1	1-2
Tottenham	3-3	1-0
West Brom	3-2	1-2
West Ham	0-2	1-2

Final League Record

P	W	D	L	F	A	Pts	Pos
42	11	7	24	54	85	29	21st

FA Cup

Rnd 3	Preston	(a)	1-0
Rnd 4	Liverpool	(a)	0-1

Football League Cup

Rnd 2	West Brom	(a)	1-6

West Brom inside-right Jeff Astle leads the Albion assualt on Villa's goal. Villa were torn to shreds in this League Cup tie in September 1966, losing 6-1 at the Hawthorns.

The goal that spelled relegation for Villa. Withers punches into his own net to give Burnley victory in April 1967.

1967-8

Naturally enough, Aston Villa started the season with a new manager — the former Burnley centre-half, Tommy Cummings, who had been managing Mansfield Town. In fact, Villa had been managerless since before the last game of the previous season when Dick Taylor and his entire coaching staff were axed. Taylor, along with his assistants and former Villa players Bill Baxter and Johnny Dixon, was out of a job even before that 6–2 humiliation at The Dell. Cummings came to Villa Park full of optimism and hope that he could steer Villa back into the First Division at the first attempt. After all, although the club had been twice before relegated, they had always bounced back within a season or two at the most. Yet for much of 1967-8, Villa fans feared that their team might actually go down to the Third Division.

At the beginning of October, Villa were in the bottom four of the Second Division and deep in trouble once again. Morale was low in the players'

camp and Colin Withers, John Sleeuwenhoek, and Mick Wright had each asked for a transfer out of Villa Park as soon as possible. Sleeuwenhoek and Wright were granted their requests straight away.

Cummings also bought in players and of these, Brian Godfrey ended the season as Villa's top scorer with thirteen goals. Two others, Brian Greenhalgh and Tommy Mitchinson — who Cummings had bought from Mansfield — scored a combined total of twenty-one goals and so the Villa boss could be pleased with his signings.

Cummings also bought Mike Tindall, the ex-Spurs player, and Willie Anderson, the Manchester United outside-left who had spent much of his time in the reserve side at Old Trafford. Second Division soccer was better than Central League football with a First Division club and Anderson agreed to join Villa for a fee of £20,000

With these new players, and with some of the staff that he had inherited, Cummings set about rescuing Villa from what many supporters saw as a fate worse than death. At the end of the season, Cummings had done a good enough job and Villa were safe —

Norwich City manage to clear this attack led by Brian Greenhalgh but Villa still won 4-2.

Villa's Brian Godfrey manages to get the ball into the Blackburn net but the effort is disallowed for a foul on Ronnie Clayton (on the ground). Blackburn won 2-1 in March 1968.

Second Division results 1967-8

	H	A
Birmingham	2-4	1-2
Blackburn	1-2	1-2
Blackpool	3-2	0-1
Bolton	1-1	3-2
Bristol City	2-4	0-0
Cardiff	2-1	0-3
Carlisle	1-0	2-1
Charlton	4-1	0-3
Crystal Palace	0-1	1-0
Derby	2-1	1-3
Huddersfield	0-0	0-0
Hull	2-3	0-3
Ipswich	2-2	1-2
Middlesbrough	0-1	1-1
Millwall	3-1	2-1
Norwich	4-2	0-1
Plymouth	0-1	1-2
Portsmouth	1-0	2-2
Preston	1-0	1-2
QPR	1-2	0-3
Rotherham	3-1	2-0

Final League Record

P	W	D	L	F	A	Pts	Pos
42	15	7	20	54	64	37	16th

FA Cup

Rnd 3	Millwall	(h)	3-0
Rnd 4	Rotherham	(h)	0-1

Football League Cup

Rnd 2	Northampton	(a)	1-3

although sixteenth place in the Second Division was not the kind of position that the club's fans could get used to. There were unfamiliar trips to Plymouth, Rotherham and Carlisle, all Second Division outposts, and Villa fans missed the bubble and excitement of Old Trafford and Highbury.

Another cause for concern was that Villa's average gate had fallen to some 16,000. Within many supporters' living memories, it had been 40,000. Third Division Northampton Town beat Villa 3-1 at Northampton in the second round of the Football League Cup, and after beating Millwall 3-0 in the FA Cup, Villa were dumped out 1-0 at home to Rotherham.

Cummings enlisted the aid of former West Ham star Malcolm Musgrove as his coach and he gave the first team captaincy to Lew Chatterley. He also signed another Mansfield player in defender Dick Edwards, and by the end of the season had blooded several young Villa players. Difficult years still lay ahead for Aston Villa Football Club and the signs were there as the club went into the transfer market, not for established stars, but for Third Division footballers who would 'do a job' for the club. There were dark days ahead.

1968-9

What a season! Third Division football staring Villa in the face, mounted police keeping back angry fans, boardroom takeover bids (including one from the United States), public protest meetings, and lastly, a fantastic end-of-season run in which Villa escaped relegation under one of the most colourful and controversial managers that the game has ever seen.

Matters boiled over in November of this season when Villa were stranded at the foot of the Second Division after three defeats in a row and with only eleven points from their first nineteen games. On the day that Preston North End beat Villa 1-0 at Villa Park, the Villa fans screamed for the heads of the board and the management; policemen on horseback had to move irate Villa supporters from jostling outside the ground after the game. Heads did roll but they were not those of the directors, but those of manager Tommy Cummings and his colleague Malcolm Musgrove. Earlier in the season, Cummings had appointed Arthur Cox as his new trainer and it was Cox who took over as caretaker-manager now that Cummings had been fired. There followed a mass protest meeting at Digbeth Civic Hall when the board were given an ultimatum by the fans — 'get it straight — or get out!' Meanwhile, Arthur Cox was having his own problems as Villa's Welsh international wing-half, Barry Hole, walked out after a bust-up.

There came threats to the board's survival from all manner of quarters — from Atlanta Chiefs in America, from a faction headed by Sir Frank Price, the former Lord Mayor of Birmingham, from the chairman of Walsall FC. Eventually, in December

1968, the entire Villa board resigned and a new set of directors, headed by Douglas Ellis, a Birmingham travel agent, and Pat Matthews, a financier, took control. The new board also included former Villa player Harry Parkes. Immediately they were installed, the new Villa board named former Preston, Arsenal and Scotland wing-half, Tommy Docherty, as their new manager. Docherty had just half a season to prevent Villa going into the Third Division for the first time in the club's history. He went back to one of his old clubs, Rotherham United, to buy Brian Tiler, a tough and experienced half-back. He also moved Dick Edwards from full-back to centre-half — a move which paid immediate dividends —

Second Division results 1968-9

	H	A
Birmingham	1-0	0-4
Blackburn	1-1	0-2
Blackpool	0-1	1-1
Bolton	1-1	1-4
Bristol City	1-0	0-1
Bury	1-0	2-3
Cardiff	2-0	1-1
Carlisle	0-0	1-0
Charlton	0-0	1-1
Crystal Palace	1-1	2-4
Derby	0-1	1-3
Fulham	1-1	1-1
Huddersfield	1-0	1-3
Hull	1-1	0-1
Middlesbrough	1-0	0-0
Millwall	1-1	1-0
Norwich	2-1	1-1
Oxford	2-0	0-1
Portsmouth	2-0	0-2
Preston	0-1	0-1
Sheffield Utd	3-1	1-3

Final League Record

P	W	D	L	F	A	Pts	Pos
42	12	14	16	37	48	38	18th

FA Cup

Rnd 3	QPR	(h)	2-1
Rnd 4	Southampton	(a)	2-2
Replay	Southampton	(h)	2-1
Rnd 5	Tottenham	(a)	2-3

Football League Cup

Rnd 2	Tottenham	(a)	1-4

The Aston Villa squad which came perilously near to the Third Division in 1968-9.

and when Tiler scored on his debut as Villa beat Cardiff City 2–0 at Villa Park, Docherty's faith had been repaid twice over.

Villa won five successive games in the first month of the New Year, during which time they had moved from bottom place to fifth-from-bottom. Docherty also inspired the Villa public to come flocking back. On 7 December, Villa had attracted an all-time low of 12,747 to see Charlton force a 0–0 draw at Villa Park as the Claret and Blues grovelled around the Second Division basement with the likes of Fulham, Bristol City, Oxford and Bury. Six weeks later, the crowds were pouring back.

Docherty saved Villa from relegation and also steered them to the fifth round of the FA Cup. Against Southampton in a fourth round replay, Villa won 2–1 in front of nearly 60,000 fans. Only in the last sixteen did they fall when Spurs beat them 3–2 at White Hart Lane. Before the season ended, Docherty made another signing — Arsenal's Dave Simmons — and by the end of the Easter programme, Villa were out of danger. It had been one of the most traumatic seasons in the history of Aston Villa Football Club and for weeks the club had been headline news — for all the wrong reasons. The fans felt that the club had turned a corner. They had not.

Villa's new boy Simmons joins in the celebrations as Rudge punches the air with joy after scoring the only goal of the game with Bury in February 1969.

1969-70

Of all the dark days that Aston Villa had endured in the 1950s and 1960s, this season was surely the darkest of them all. When it ended, Villa were in twenty-first place in the Second Division, two points adrift of the next club, Charlton Athletic, and heading towards the Third Division for the very first time in their history. Aston Villa in the Third Division! It seemed an incredible prospect, not only for the thousands of Villa supporters, but for the masses who followed football in general. In the cups, Villa also crashed, losing to Charlton in the third round of the FA Cup and to West Bromwich Albion in the second round of the Football League Cup.

When the season opened, work was in hand to modernise part of Villa Park, Villa had been on a close season tour to America, and new signings had been made including Ian Hamilton from Southend and Bruce and Neil Rioch from Luton Town. Everything looked set for a determined assault on the Second Division title. After half their matches had been played, Villa found themselves at the foot of the table again with only ten points — nineteen behind

the sides at the top. From then on things got even worse — if that is possible — and when the final table was drawn up, Villa had won just eight matches and had twenty-nine points. Even worse, they had scored only thirty-six goals. Docherty did not stay around to see the club's final humiliation. After the cup defeat, Vic Crowe found himself in charge of the team.

Crowe had been in America with Woosnam and Atlanta Chiefs (where Peter McParland had also ended up) and had then returned to Birmingham before Docherty gave him the chance to coach Aston Villa's Central League team. Now he was given the job of working a soccer miracle and pulling Villa — his old club — back from the brink. Villa had started the season badly — beaten 1-0 by Norwich at Villa Park on the opening day — and the pattern had been

Villa's new signing Bruce Rioch blasts the ball past Norwich City's David Stringer and Duncan Forbes. But Villa lost 1-0 at home to the Canaries in this Second Division match on the opening day of the season.

maintained. There was little that Crowe could do to halt the slide into the Third Division abyss. He had none of Docherty's undoubted flamboyance — who else would sign on a Zambian international called Freddie Mwila? — but he was a first-rate coach and his main area of discrepancy was a complete and utter lack of time. Poor Vic Crowe was given the Villa job when the side was already doomed — even if the statistics pointed out that Villa could fight their way out of the black hole in which they found themselves, there was no way in which the side could literally turn those games into points.

Between them, Docherty and Crowe called up thirty players to the Villa first team — always a sign of a struggling team; another sure sign was that

Bruce Rioch, who played in every Aston Villa game in 1969-70, had the distinction of becoming the club's leading scorer — with just *six* goals! Pat McMahon and Willie Anderson chipped in with five apiece. So Aston Villa were Third Division bound. What the ghost of George Ramsey made of it all is anyone's guess. When he brought Villa to greatness, the prospect of even having a Third Division in the Football League was unthinkable. It was a lesson to everyone in football that even the greatest names must occasionally fall and mix it with the humblest. Teams like Chesterfield, Halifax and Bradford City would be at Villa Park next season. There was even the prospect of a local derby with Walsall!

Second Division results 1969-70

	H	A
Birmingham	0-0	2-0
Blackburn	1-1	0-2
Blackpool	0-0	1-2
Bolton	3-0	1-2
Bristol City	0-2	0-1
Cardiff	1-1	0-4
Carlisle	1-0	1-1
Charlton	1-0	0-1
Huddersfield	4-1	0-2
Hull	3-2	1-3
Leicester	0-1	0-1
Middlesbrough	2-0	0-1
Millwall	2-2	0-2
Norwich	0-1	1-3
Oxford	0-0	2-2
Portsmouth	3-5	0-0
Preston	0-0	1-1
QPR	1-1	2-4
Sheffield Utd	1-0	0-5
Swindon	0-2	1-1
Watford	0-2	0-3

Final League Record

P	W	D	L	F	A	Pts	Pos
42	8	13	21	36	62	29	21st

FA Cup

Rnd 3	Charlton	(h)	1-1
Replay	Charlton	(a)	0-1

Football League Cup

Rnd 1	Chester	(a)	2-1
Rnd 2	West Brom	(h)	1-2

15-year-old Jim Brown, Villa's Scottish schoolboy international who became the youngest-ever player to appear for the club in a league match, when he made his debut against Bolton Wanderers in 1969-70.

1970-1

Even from the Third Division, Villa gave their fans something to cheer about. Although they missed promotion, Villa marched back to another Football League Cup final and although that was ultimately lost, there could not have been a Villa supporter who even considered the possibility of Wembley as the season got underway with a League match at Chesterfield. Even so, Villa took £50,000 in advance ticket sales during the summer of 1970 to underline Tommy Docherty's famous remark: 'We'd get five thousand turn up to watch the shirts dry at Villa Park!'

Crowe began his first full season in charge of Villa with a new assistant, as Stuart Williams left for foreign shores, and former Villa star Ron Wylie moved over from St Andrew's to rejoin his old club. Villa started the season with a 3–2 win at Saltergate and in their first thirteen League games they lost only once — a shock 1–0 home defeat by Mansfield Town. Up until their appearance in the Football League Cup final, Villa looked strong promotion candidates as they fought out the top placings with Preston and Fulham (subsequently promoted), Halifax, Chesterfield and Bristol Rovers. After Wembley, Villa fell away badly and they won only five points from the six games which followed the final. The gap between Villa and the top clubs increased rapidly and they left themselves with no chance of catching up and finished in fourth place, seven points short of promotion.

For the first time in their history Villa were obliged to enter the earliest stages of the FA Cup, so far as Football League teams are concerned, and in the first round match against fellow Third Division side Torquay United on 21 November, Villa lost 3–1 at Plainmoor with their solitary goal coming from Charlie Aitken.

Villa also found themselves in the first round of the League Cup and here they soon accounted for Notts County, beating the Fourth Division champions elect, 4–0; it was the start of the Wembley march and Burnley, Northampton, Carlisle and Bristol Rovers all fell in Villa's path, although Northampton and Rovers each forced replays. Villa fans could hardly wait for the semi-final draw and when it paired their club with mighty Manchester

Aston Villa players who had the doubtful privilege of being the first ever to play for the club in the Third Division.

Third Division results 1970-1

Aug 15   Chesterfield   (a)   3–2
(McMahon, B. Rioch 2; 16,750)
Aug 22   Plymouth   (h)   1–1
(McMahon; 29,205)
Aug 29   Swansea   (a)   2–1
(Hamilton, McMahon; 13,535)
Aug 31   Mansfield   (h)   0–1
(30,856)
Sep   5   Doncaster   (h)   3–2
(Lochhead 2, McMahon; 23,602)
Sep 12   Barnsley   (a)   1–1
(Simmons; 13,408)
Sep 19   Preston   (h)   2–0
(Lochhead 2; 26,139)
Sep 23   Gillingham   (h)   2–1
(Hamilton, McMahon; 29,388)
Sep 26   Wrexham   (a)   3–2
(Lochhead, Gibson, Hamilton pen; 18,335)
Sep 30   Bristol Rov   (h)   1–1
(Lochhead; 32,082)
Oct   3   Brighton   (h)   0–0
(26,189)
Oct 10   Rochdale   (a)   1–1
(Lochhead; 7,634)
Oct 17   Chesterfield   (h)   0–0
(27,049)
Oct 19   Port Vale   (a)   0–2
(11,224)
Oct 24   Tranmere   (h)   1–0
(Hamilton; 20,676)
Oct 31   Reading   (a)   5–3
(Lochhead, Tiler, Butler own goal, McMahon,
Anderson pen; 13,312)
Nov   7   Torquay   (h)   0–1
(28,099)
Nov 11   Bury   (h)   1–0
(Hamilton; 17,014)
Nov 14   Halifax   (a)   1–2
(Turnbull; 5,845)
Nov 28   Fulham   (a)   2–0
(Hamilton, McMahon; 16,021)
Dec   5   Bradford City   (h)   1–0
(Hamilton; 23,623)
Dec 19   Plymouth A   (a)   1–1
(Lochhead; 12,996)
Dec 26   Shrewsbury   (h)   2–0
(McMahon, B. Rioch; 31,186)
Jan   2   Walsall   (a)   0–3
(19,203)
Jan   9   Bristol R   (a)   2–1
(B. Rioch, Parsons own goal; 25,836)
Jan 16   Port Vale   (h)   1–0
(B. Rioch; 28,965)
Jan 23   Rotherham   (a)   1–1
(Hamilton; 12,648)

Jan 30   Fulham   (h)   1–0
(Anderson pen; 33,343)
Feb   6   Bradford City   (a)   0–1
(4,840)
Feb 13   Rotherham   (h)   1–0
(Anderson; 27,183)
Feb 20   Bury   (a)   1–3
(Allen own goal; 7,516)
Mar   5   Tranmere   (a)   1–1
(Hamilton; 6,579)
Mar 10   Gillingham   (a)   0–0
(10,812)
Mar 13   Halifax   (h)   1–1
(Turnbull; 33,522)
Mar 17   Walsall   (h)   0–0
(37,642)
Mar 20   Torquay Utd   (a)   1–1
(Vowden; 6,792)
Mar 26   Doncaster   (a)   1–2
(Gregory; 7,879)
Apr   3   Swansea   (h)   3–0
(Vowden 2, Gregory; 23,571)
Apr   8   Brighton   (a)   0–1
(22,687)
Apr 10   Shrewsbury   (a)   1–2
(Turnbull; 13,636)
Apr 12   Barnsley   (h)   0–0
(20,700)
Apr 17   Rochdale   (h)   1–0
(Vowden; 18,389)
Apr 24   Preston   (a)   0–0
(22,616)
Apr 26   Mansfield   (a)   0–2
(9,666)
May   1   Wrexham   (h)   3–4
(Vowden, Godfrey 2; 18,733)
May   4   Reading   (h)   2–1
(Anderson, Bell own goal; 16,666)

Final League Record

P	W	D	L	F	A	Pts	Pos
46	19	15	12	54	46	53	4th

League Goalscorers; Hamilton 9, Lochhead 9,
McMahon 8, B. Rioch 5, Vowden 5, Anderson 4,
Turnbull 3, Gregory 2, Godfrey 2, Martin 1, Gibson
1, Simmons 1, Tiler 1, Opp own goals 3.

FA Cup

Nov 21   (Rnd 1) Torquay   (a)   1–3
(Aitken; 9,227)
FA Cup goalscorer: Aitken

Football League Cup

Aug 17 (Rnd 1) Notts Co (h) 4-0
(Anderson, McMahon, B. Rioch, Hamilton; 17,843)
Sep 9 (Rnd 2) Burnley (h) 2-0
(Hamilton, Martin; 28,341)
Oct 6 (Rnd 3) Northampton (a) 1-1
(Hamilton; 15,072)
Oct 13 (Replay) Northampton (h) 3-0
(Lochhead 2, Anderson; 25,822)
Oct 28 (Rnd 4) Carlisle (h) 1-0
(Tiler; 26,779)
Nov 17 (Rnd 5) Bristol Rov (a) 1-1
(McMahon; 28,780)
Nov 25 (Replay) Bristol Rov (h) 1-0
(McMahon; 36,483)
Dec 16 (SF 1 leg) Man Utd (a) 1-1
(Lochhead; 49,000)
Dec 23 (SF 2nd leg) Man Utd (h) 2-1
(Lochhead, McMahon; 62,500)
Villa won 3-2 on aggregate
Feb 27 (Final) Tottenham (Wembley) 0-2
(100,000)

Football League Cup Goalscorers: Lochhead 4,
McMahon 4, Hamilton 3, Anderson 2, B. Rioch 1,
Tiler 1, Martin 1.

United, 8,000 of them treked to Old Trafford for the first-leg and were rewarded with a 2-1 win. Andy Lochhead scored the first after forty minutes and although Kidd equalised shortly afterwards, the result was good enough. At Villa Park seven days later, Villa gave United a goal start and then fought back through Lochhead and McMahon to reach Wembley. United were falling from grace but their name was still held in awe and when McMahon's late header put Villa through, all football applauded them.

Tottenham Hotspur won the 1971 Football League Cup against Aston Villa, but Villa gave a good account of themselves although it was obvious that even their enthusiasm and drive was no ultimate match for a First Division side. Even so, Villa had two chances to win the game before Spurs scored late in the game. Andy Lochhead missed an open goal, allowing Spurs to get back and clear his half-hit shot; and Ian Hamilton clipped the bar with a rasping, rising shot with Jenning well beaten. Martin Chivers had been well-shackled by Turnbull all afternoon, but twice in the last twelve minutes of the game, he escaped and scored the goals which gave Spurs the trophy. Villa and Vic Crowe had faced a difficult season and they had coped well, however, as Villa fans were again given something about which to cheer.

Spurs Martin Chivers scores the first of his two goals against Villa in the 1971 League Cup final at Wembley.

1971-2

The season that Aston Villa came back! After steadying themselves in the uncharted waters of the Third Division the previous season, Villa knew which way to go and, more important, how to get there without foundering. With a few new faces in the team, and with the knowledge gained from the previous campaign, Vic Crowe brought Villa back through on the first leg of their journey back to the top drawer of English football.

In the close season of 1971, Crowe released one Villa stalwart in exchange for a player who was to help spearhead his plans. Villa's captain, Brian Godfrey, went to Eastville while Bristol Rovers striker Ray Graydon made the opposite journey to Villa Park. Graydon was to score thirteen vital goals in Villa's push out of the doldrums and although Godfrey's move was to be an unpopular one with the fans, it was the only way that Crowe could ensure he secured the signature of Graydon. Other new faces included Chelsea's goalkeeper, Tommy Hughes, although he was soon replaced by Jim Cumbes from West Bromwich Albion, and from Birmingham City came wing-half Malcolm Beard. With Godfrey departed, Crowe turned to Harry Gregory to lead Villa. Signed from Charlton Athletic in 1970-1, Gregory took to his new responsibilities well and he was a mainstay of Villa's useful start to the season.

Plymouth came to Villa Park on the first day of 1971-2 and were beaten 3–1; there followed a 1–1 draw with Walsall — a game which surprisingly attracted only 13,000 — and then a 2–0 win at home to Rochdale before Villa lost their first game at Bolton. Brighton were the next visitors to Villa Park and Villa beat their promotion rivals 2–0. By this time Bruce Rioch regained the Villa captaincy and at the end of October — with Rioch's younger brother Neil in the side, Villa beat Blackburn 4–1 with the younger Rioch scoring twice. Again Villa went out of the FA Cup at the first attempt — this time beaten by Fourth Division promotion seekers, Southend United, but by the turn of the year wins over Oldham, Bradford City, Bolton and Swansea had eased them up the table until a win over Barnsley in mid-January gave Villa the lead. On 12 February, the Third Division attendance record was broken when 48,110 saw Villa beat Bournemouth 2–1 at Villa Park.

After netting £35,000 from a match with Brazilian aces Santos — Pele and all — Villa bought Ian Ross from Liverpool for £70,000 and the midfielder made his debut in the 2–0 win over Port Vale. Five days after an important 3–0 win over Notts County at

It's there! Villa's Geoff Vowden leaps over Plymouth goalkeeper Jim Furnell after scoring Villa's first goal of the season.

Meadow Lane, Crowe went into the transfer market again and paid Luton £90,000 for centre-half Chris Nicholl. Thus strengthened, Villa forged ahead and although they lost 2–1 to Brighton on 25 March, promotion was gained five points ahead of the Sussex club. On 24 April, Villa clinched promotion by drawing 1–1 at Mansfield's Field Mill. Five days later, Villa were the champions after a 5–1 home win over Torquay United and when they beat Chesterfield 1–0 on the last day of the season, Villa had established a new Third Division record of seventy points. Villa also played seven matches in the League Cup but got only as far as the fourth round after replays against Wrexham and Crystal Palace; and the youth side won the FA Youth Cup. But the really important thing was that Villa were no longer a Third Division club.

Third Division results 1971-2

Aug 14 Plymouth (h) 3–1
(Vowden, McMahon, Anderson pen; 26,327)
Aug 21 Walsall (a) 1–1
(Vowden; 13,051)
Aug 28 Rochdale (h) 2–0
(Lochhead, Graydon; 24,272)
Sep 4 Bolton (a) 0–2
(11,470)
Sep 11 Brighton (h) 2–0
(Graydon, Hamilton; 25,809)
Sep 18 Halifax (a) 1–0
(Graydon; 7,462)
Sep 22 Mansfield (h) 0–1
(28,106)
Sep 25 Wrexham (h) 2–0
(Anderson pen, May own goal; 22,997)
Sep 28 Barnsley (a) 4–0
(Lochhead 2, Hamilton 2; 8,387)
Oct 2 Bristol Rovers (a) 1–0
(Anderson; 20,428)
Oct 9 Rotherham (h) 1–2
(Lochhead; 30,249)
Oct 16 Plymouth (a) 2–3
(B. Rioch, Vowden; 18,570)
Oct 20 Tranmere (h) 2–0
(B. Rioch, Lochhead; 24,231)
Oct 23 Bournemouth (a) 0–3
(20,305)
Oct 30 Blackburn (h) 4–1
(N. Rioch 2, Hamilton, Anderson; 25,588)
Nov 6 Port Vale (a) 4–4
(Hamilton, Anderson pen, Cross own goal, Graydon; 11,106)
Nov 13 Notts County (h) 1–0
(Graydon; 37,462)
Nov 27 Oldham (a) 6–0
(Lochhead 3, Anderson, B. Rioch 2; 12,015)

Dec 4 Bradford City (h) 3–0
(Anderson pen, B. Rioch 2; 27,847)
Dec 18 Bolton (h) 3–2
(Lochhead, Graydon, Aitken; 27,767)
Dec 27 Swansea (a) 2–1
(Aitken, Graydon; 24,419)
Jan 1 Halifax (h) 1–0
(Graydon; 32,749)
Jan 8 Rochdale (a) 0–1
(5,871)
Jan 19 Shrewsbury (h) 3–0
(Hamilton, Graydon, Lochhead; 27,239)
Jan 22 Barnsley (h) 2–0
(Lochhead, B. Rioch; 30,531)
Jan 28 Tranmere (a) 1–0
(Aitken; 12,054)
Feb 5 York (h) 1–0
(Anderson pen; 26,905)
Feb 12 Bournemouth (h) 2–1
(Vowden, Lochhead; 48,110)
Feb 19 Blackburn (a) 1–1
(Lochhead; 15,562)
Feb 26 Port Vale (h) 2–0
(Lochhead, McMahon; 32,806)
Mar 4 Notts County (a) 3–0
(McMahon 2, Graydon; 34,208)
Mar 11 Rotherham (a) 2–0
(Lochhead, Graydon; 16,290)
Mar 15 Shrewsbury (a) 1–1
(Nicholl; 16,000)
Mar 18 Walsall (h) 0–0
(45,953)
Mar 25 Brighton (a) 1–2
(B. Rioch; 29,135)
Mar 31 Wrexham (a) 2–0
(Anderson, Graydon; 16,846)
Apr 1 Swansea (h) 2–0
(Anderson, McMahon; 33,394)
Apr 3 Bristol Rovers (h) 2–1
(Lochhead 2; 41,518)
Apr 8 York (a) 1–0
(B Rioch; 9,620)
Apr 10 Oldham (h) 1–0
(Graydon; 32,140)
Apr 12 Torquay (a) 1–2
(Vowden; 9,776)
Apr 19 Chesterfield (a) 4–0
(Lochhead, Vowden 2, Hamilton; 12,510)
Apr 22 Bradford City (a) 1–0
(Aitken; 9,285)
Apr 24 Mansfield (a) 1–1
(Vowden; 12,454)
Apr 29 Torquay (h) 5–1
(Vowden 2, Lochhead, Jackson own goal, Little; 37,582)
May 5 Chesterfield (h) 1–0
(Ross; 45,567)

Final League Record

P	W	D	L	F	A	Pts	Pos
46	32	6	8	85	32	70	1st

Football League Goalscorers: Lochhead 19, Graydon 13, Anderson 10, Vowden 10, B. Rioch 9, Hamilton 7, McMahon 5, Aitken 4, N. Rioch 2, Little 1, Ross 1, Nicholl 1, own goals 3.

FA Cup

Nov 20 (Rnd 1) Southend (a) 0–1
(16,929)

Football League Cup

Aug 18 (Rnd 1) Wrexham (h) 2–2
(Lochhead, Anderson pen; 24,552)

Aug 23 (Replay) Wrexham (a) 1–1
(Anderson; 12,113)

Aug 31 (Replay) Wrexham (n) 4–3
(Lochhead 2, Anderson pen, Ingle own goal; 20,697)

Sep 8 (Rnd 2) Chesterfield (a) 3–2
(Lochhead, Vowden, Anderson; 15,000)

Oct 5 (Rnd 3) Crystal P. (a) 2–2
(Hamilton, Lochhead; 21,179)

Oct 13 (Replay) Crystal P. (h) 2–0
(Lochhead, Graydon; 24,978)

Oct 26 (Rnd 4) Blackpool (a) 1–4
(Anderson; 20,193)

Football League Cup Goalscorers: Lochhead 6, Anderson 5, Graydon, Hamilton, Vowden, Opp own goal.

Andy Lochhead gets a header past the Crystal Palace defence as Villa win this League Cup 3rd round replay 2-0 in October 1971.

1972-3

There is no doubt that Aston Villa's achievement in finishing third in their first season back in the Second Division was a fine one indeed. Although they were eleven points behind second club Queens Park Rangers, it is also to be remembered that in subsequent seasons, third place is good enough to bring First Division soccer. In fact, the rules were changed only twelve months after Villa missed out.

Yet before the season had even started there was yet another boardroom battle and public meetings which, I suppose, served to show what passions Aston Villa arouse, so great a club are they. This particular battle resulted in Harry Parkes losing his seat to former Test cricketer Alan Smith, although Doug Ellis hung on to his position as a director. There was yet another upheaval in October when Doug Ellis was elected chairman and former Villa player and manager, Eric Houghton, was made a director, with Dick Greenhalgh and Bob Mackay losing their seats. Then Harry Kartz, who had resigned because of business committments, was reinstated and at the end of the season, Sir William

Charlie Aitken played 33 league games in 1972-3 to bring his total nearer to Billy Walker's record of 480. Eventually Aitken eclipsed Walker's total.

Second Division results 1972-3

Aug 12 Preston (a) 1-0
(Anderson; 17,371)

Aug 19 Huddersfield (h) 2-0
(Vowden, Graydon; 34,843)

Aug 26 Burnley (a) 1-4
(Hamilton; 14,804)

Aug 29 Carlisle (h) 1-0
(B. Rioch; 29,047)

Sep 2 Brighton (h) 1-1
(Lochhead; 30,175)

Sep 9 Cardiff (a) 2-0
(B. Rioch, Lochhead; 15,729)

Sep 16 Swindon (h) 2-1
(Evans, Lochhead; 30,775)

Sep 23 Nottm Forest (a) 1-1
(Cottam own goal; 18,082)

Sep 27 Sunderland (h) 2-0
(Evans, B. Rioch; 29,895)

Sep 30 Millwall (h) 1-0
(B. Rioch pen; 31,524)

Oct 7 Fulham (a) 0-2
(17,576)

Oct 14 QPR (h) 0-1
(34,045)

Oct 17 Blackpool (a) 1-1
(Evans; 15,043)

Oct 21 Portsmouth (a) 1-0
(Vowden; 13,524)

Oct 28 Middlesbrough (h) 1-1
(Vowden; 30,048)

Nov 4 Sunderland (a) 2-2
(B. Rioch, Little; 18,717)

Nov 11 Blackpool (h) 0-0
(31,651)

Nov 18 Luton (h) 0-2
(29,144)

Nov 25 Oxford Utd (a) 0-2
(13,412)

Dec 2 Hull (h) 2-0
(Graydon pen, Hamilton; 21,213)

Dec 16 Orient (h) 1-0
(Evans; 20,572)

Dec 23 Sheff Wed (a) 2-2
(Graydon 2; 20,961)

Dec 26 Nottm Forest (h) 2-2
(Lochhead, Evans; 37,000)

Dec 30 Huddersfield (a) 1-1
(Evans; 9,719)

Jan 6 Burnley (h) 0-3
(38,637)

Jan 20 Brighton (a) 3-1
(Evans, Graydon, Brown; 12,212)

Jan 27 Cardiff (h) 2-0
(Graydon pen, B. Rioch; 28,856)

Feb 10 Swindon (a) 3-1
(Evans, Graydon 2; 13,615)

Feb 17 Preston (h) 1-1
(Aitken; 27,717)

Feb 24 Orient (a) 0-4
(9,085)

Mar 3 Fulham (h) 2-3
(Little, B. Rioch; 24,007)

Mar 10 QPR (a) 0-1
(21,578)

Mar 17 Portsmouth (h) 2-0
(Vowden, McMahon; 18,432)

Mar 24 Middlesbrough (a) 1-1
(McMahon; 9,776)

Mar 27 Bristol City (a) 0-3
(15,654)

Mar 31 Oxford Utd (h) 2-1
(McMahon, Vowden; 15,902)

Apr 7 Hull City (a) 2-1
(Brown, Little; 8,072)

Apr 14 Bristol City (h) 1-0
(N. Rioch; 19,545)

Apr 21 Luton (a) 0-0
(10,971)

Apr 23 Millwall (a) 1-1
(Graydon; 9,768)

Apr 24 Sheff Wed (h) 2-1
(Lochhead, Hamilton; 20,710)

Apr 28 Carlisle (a) 2-2
(Lochhead, Hamilton; 6,178)

Final League Record

P	W	D	L	F	A	Pts	Pos
42	18	14	10	51	47	50	3rd

Football League Goalscorers: Graydon 9, Evans 8, B. Rioch 7, Lochhead 6, Vowden 5, Hamilton 4, Little 3, McMahon 3, Brown 2, Anderson 1, Aitken 1, N. Rioch 1, Opp own goal 1.

FA Cup

Jan 13 (Rnd 3) Everton (a) 2-3
(Vowden, Evans; 42,222)

FA Cup Goalscoers: Vowden, Evans

Football League Cup

Aug 16 (Rnd 1) Hereford (h) 4-1
(Rioch, Graydon, Vowden, Evans; 32,314)

Sep 5 (Rnd 2) Nottm Forest (a) 1-0
(Evans; 17,665)

Oct 4 (Rnd 3) Leeds (h) 1-1
(B. Rioch; 46,185)

Oct 11 (Replay) Leeds (a) 0-2
(28,894)

Football League Cup Goalscorers: B. Rioch 2, Evans 2, Graydon, Vowden.

Ray Graydon only scored nine goals in 1972-3 — but he finished the season as Villa's leading scorer.

Dugdale and Harry Cressman joined the board in the never-ending game of Aston Villa musical chairs.

On the field, Villa also had changes during the close season when Alun Evans, the former Wolves young star, joined Villa from Liverpool for £75,000. Two wins in their first two matches gave Villa a great start, coupled with a Football League Cup win over Hereford. But then Burnley won 4–1 at Turf Moor and this result brought Villa's thoughts of a quick return to the First Division down to earth.

By the middle of October, Villa were out of the Football League Cup, beaten 2–0 at Elland Road after drawing 1–1 with Leeds at Villa Park before 46,000 fans. The FA Cup also brought little cheer, although Villa did have the chance of going straight into the third round drawing, now that they were a Second Division club again. However, it did them little good as Everton beat them 3–2 at Goodison Park, although Villa played well enough to merit that tight scoreline. Just before the Villa-Everton tie, Vic Crowe bought Derby County's young full-back, John Robson, for £90,000. Robson was to give Villa a good few seasons before his career was sadly halted by a serious illness. The turn of the year was a good time from Villa's point of view — at least so far as the Second Division programme went — and they enjoyed wins over Brighton, Cardiff and Swindon to take them well into February.

However, they were never really in contention for the top two places and the end of the season brought this table:

	P	W	D	L	F	A	Pts
1 Burnley	42	24	14	4	72	35	62
2 QPR	42	24	13	5	81	37	61
3 Aston Villa	42	18	14	10	51	47	50

So Villa would have to spend at least one more season — it turned out to be two — in the Second Division.

1973-4

Although Aston Villa had lost that ever-consistent goalscorer, Andy Lochhead, to Oldham Athletic, the club really felt that 1973-4 was going to be their season for promotion. Crowe had made two useful signings in Welsh international Trevor Hockey and Irish international Sammy Morgan, and at the end of September, Villa were unbeaten and stood nicely placed in fourth spot. There followed two away defeats at the hands of Notts County and Fulham before Villa got back to form with a 5-0 trouncing of Cardiff City at Villa Park. By the middle of November, Villa were in third place, two points behind the second club Orient. Suddenly, Villa slipped and fell. Five defeats and a draw in six games pushed them right down the table.

The rot started when Hull managed a glum 1-1 draw at Villa Park and this was followed by defeats at the hands of Swindon, Sunderland, Luton, West Brom and Oxford. Only a 1-1 draw with Notts County gave Villa any profit in that time. It was 23 February before Villa won another game — when they beat Cardiff 1-0 at Ninian Park. Cardiff were to miss relegation only by goal average and Villa's win could not be described as a turning point for them. In thirteen games Villa had scored only five goals and this actually put them into the fringe of the relegation struggle instead of in the heat of the promotion race. There were several reasons for the demise, not least the failure of some players to produce their true form at the crucial time. Ray Graydon and Bruce Rioch were also suffering from injuries and in the final analysis, that awful spell of bad results left Villa a slightly below average Second Division club when the season ended.

York City knocked Villa out of the League Cup, 1-0 at Bootham Crescent, but in the FA Cup, the club had its share of the glory, including an epic 2-0 win over Arsenal in the fourth round at Villa Park after the sides had drawn 1-1 at Highbury. In the first game, Morgan was sent off after a challenge on Arsenal goalkeeper, Bob Wilson, and Villa hung on with ten men after having earlier taken the lead through the Irishman. In the replay, nearly 48,000 fans saw Villa make no mistake. Morgan got his revenge by heading Villa in front before half-time and after the interval, Evans found his goal touch to make the score 2-0. Alas, high-flying Burnley put an end to Villa's Wembley hopes in the next round when they won 1-0 at Turf Moor. Villa had hoped that their centenary year would be celebrated with a return to First Division football. In the end, they had learned enough lessons to make sure that the celebrations would not be long delayed.

Oh no! Villa goalkeeper Jim Cumbes can only watch as Norman Piper's shot puts Portsmouth ahead. But Villa fought back to win 4-1 in March 1974.

Second Division results 1973-4

Aug 25 Preston (h) 2-0
(Aitken, Hockey; 28,861)
Sep 1 Millwall (a) 1-1
(Little; 12,009)
Sep 8 Oxford (h) 2-0
(B. Rioch pen, Vowden; 28,078)
Sep 11 Crystal P (a) 0-0
(20,858)
Sep 15 Middlesbrough (a) 0-0
(19,656)
Sep 19 Fulham (h) 1-1
(B. Rioch; 30,162)
Sep 22 Orient (h) 2-2
(B. Rioch, Vowden; 26,685)
Sep 29 Notts County (a) 0-2
(15,872)
Oct 2 Fulham (a) 0-1
(11,776)
Oct 6 Cardiff (h) 5-0
(Woodruff own goal, Graydon, B. Rioch 2, Morgan; 24,473)
Oct 13 Bolton (a) 2-1
(Evans 2; 19,206)
Oct 20 Bristol City (h) 2-2
(Little, Graydon; 26,918)
Oct 23 Crystal P (h) 2-1
(Little, Graydon; 26,670)
Oct 27 Nottm Forest (a) 2-1
(Graydon, Aitken; 17,718)
Nov 3 Sheff Wed (h) 1-0
(Little; 28,559)
Nov 10 Portsmouth (a) 0-2
(12,678)
Nov 17 Hull (h) 1-1
(Little; 23,773)
Nov 24 Swindon (a) 0-1
(8,476)
Dec 8 Sunderland (a) 0-2
(20,784)
Dec 15 Luton (a) 0-1
(10,020)
Dec 22 Notts County (h) 1-1
(B. Rioch; 20,825)
Dec 26 West Brom (a) 0-2
(43,080)
Dec 29 Oxford (a) 1-2
(Graydon; 10,149)
Jan 1 Millwall (h) 0-0
(20,905)
Jan 12 Middlesbrough (h) 1-1
(B. Rioch; 26,906)
Jan 19 Preston (a) 0-0
(10,766)
Feb 2 Luton (h) 0-1
(26,180)
Feb 23 Cardiff (a) 1-0
(Graydon; 12,310)
Feb 27 Bolton (h) 1-1
(McMahon; 18,952)
Mar 2 West Brom (h) 1-3
(Morgan; 37,323)
Mar 13 Carlisle (h) 2-1
(Evans, Hamilton pen; 12,007)
Mar 16 Bristol City (a) 1-0
(Morgan; 12,759)
Mar 23 Portsmouth (h) 4-1
(McMahon 2, Morgan 2; 15,517)
Apr 1 Sheff Wed (a) 4-2
(Little 2, McMahon, Leonard; 22,094)
Apr 6 Swindon (h) 1-1
(Little; 20,709)
Apr 13 Hull City (a) 1-1
(Deere own goal; 7,810)
Apr 15 Blackpool (h) 0-1
(18,351)
Apr 16 Blackpool (a) 1-2
(Hamilton; 10,787)
Apr 20 Sunderland (h) 1-2
(McMahon; 17,321)
Apr 24 Nottm Forest (h) 3-1
(Hamilton, Campbell, Graydon; 12,439)
Apr 27 Carlisle (a) 0-2
(12,494)
May 3 Orient (a) 1-1
(Graydon pen; 29,766)

Final League Record

P	W	D	L	F	A	Pts	Pos
42	13	15	14	48	45	41	14th

Football League Goalscorers: Little 8, Graydon 8, B. Rioch 7, Morgan 5, McMahon 5, Evans 3, Hamilton 3, Aitken 2, Vowden 2, Hockey 1, Leonard 1, Campbell 1. Opp own goals 2.

FA Cup

Jan 5 (Rnd 3) Chester (h) 3-1
(Nicholl, Morgan 2; 16,545)
Jan 26 (Rnd 4) Arsenal (a) 1-1
(Morgan; 41,682)
Jan 30 (Replay) Arsenal (h) 2-0
(Morgan, Evans; 47,821)
Feb 16 (Rnd 5) Burnley (a) 0-1
(29,301)

FA Cup Goalscorers: Morgan 4, Nicholl, Evans

Football League Cup

Oct 9 (Rnd 2) York City (a) 0-1
(8,000)

Flat out — that's Jim Cumbes after an all-action FA Cup tie with Arsenal in January 1974. Alan Ball looks away in disgust.

1974-5

In June 1974, Aston Villa appointed their sixth manager in ten turbulent years. Former Norwich and Manchester City manager, Ron Saunders, became the latest boss at Villa Park in place of Vic Crowe. Crowe had got Villa out of the Third Division but it appeared that he could not obtain them promotion from the Second. The events of the 1973-4 season had left the Villa board with the feeling that they must look for a new man. And Saunders, a former forward with Portsmouth, and a man who had the reputation of something of a disciplinarian, was that person. Not only did Saunders win Villa back their long-cherished First Division status, he also steered them to the Football League Cup final at Wembley where they won the trophy; and he also took the club into the fifth round of the FA Cup where they were narrowly beaten at Ipswich.

Manchester United were making an appearance in the Second Division fixture list this season after their manager, the former Villa boss, Tommy Docherty, had failed to halt their slide from the top. It was a slide which had begun with Villa beating United in

the League Cup semi-final some seasons earlier. Happily, both clubs would be reinstated in the immediate future. When the two sides met in the League in 1974-5, honours were shared with United winning 2-1 at Old Trafford in November and Villa triumphing 2-1 at Villa Park in February. The two matches were watched by a total of over 94,000 people.

United finally took the Championship like this:

		P	W	D	L	F	A	Pts
1	Manchester Utd	42	26	9	7	66	30	61
2	Aston Villa	42	25	8	9	69	32	58
3	Norwich City	42	20	13	9	58	37	53

In the Football League Cup, Villa enjoyed a splendid second round win over Everton after drawing 1-1 at Villa Park. Their 3-0 win at Goodison was one of the shocks of the season. In the

Ray Graydon scores the winning goal from the penalty spot as Villa lift the League Cup against Norwich at Wembley on 1 March 1975.

Second Division results 1974-5

Aug 17 York (a) 1–1
(Graydon; 8,740)
Aug 20 Hull (a) 1–1
(Robson; 8,712)
Aug 24 Norwich (h) 1–1
(Graydon; 23,297)
Aug 28 Hull (h) 6–0
(Morgan 3, Graydon, B. Little, Hamilton; 18,973)
Aug 31 Bolton (a) 0–1
(12,976)
Sep 7 Orient (h) 3–1
(Morgan, Graydon 2; 16,902)
Sep 14 Bristol Rovers (a) 0–2
(14,035)
Sep 21 Millwall (h) 3–0
(Graydon 3; 21,375)
Sep 28 Southampton (a) 0–0
(18,599)
Oct 2 Nottm Forest (h) 3–0
(Graydon, Hamilton, Leonard; 20,357)
Oct 5 Oldham (a) 2–1
(Hicks own goal, Graydon; 15,574)
Oct 12 Blackpool (h) 1–0
(Graydon; 25,763)
Oct 19 Sunderland (a) 0–0
(33,232)
Oct 26 Sheff Wed (h) 3–1
(Phillips, Nicholl, Graydon; 23,977)
Nov 2 Fulham (a) 1–3
(B. Little; 10,979)
Nov 9 Notts County (h) 0–1
(22,182)
Nov 16 Man United (a) 1–2
(Hamilton; 55,615)
Nov 23 Portsmouth (h) 2–0
(Hamilton, B. Little; 16,827)
Nov 29 Oxford United (h) 0–0
(18,554)
Dec 7 Bristol City (a) 0–1
(13,390)
Dec 14 York City (h) 4–0
(Graydon, B. Little, Nicholl, Hamilton; 15,840)
Dec 21 West Brom (a) 0–2
(28,011)
Dec 26 Bristol Rovers (h) 1–0
(Graydon; 21,556)
Dec 28 Cardiff (a) 1–3
(Hamilton; 11,040)
Jan 11 Bristol City (h) 2–0
(B. Little, Hamilton; 21,762)

Jan 18 Oxford United (a) 2–1
(B. Little, Nicholl; 9,872)
Feb 1 Notts County (a) 3–1
(B. Little 2, Carrodus; 17,235)
Feb 8 Fulham (h) 1–1
(Nicholl; 28,533)
Feb 18 Portsmouth (a) 3–2
(Carrodus, Graydon, B. Little; 13,355)
Feb 22 Man United (h) 2–0
(Graydon, Aitken; 39,156)
Mar 5 Bolton (h) 0–0
(39,322)
Mar 8 Nottm Forest (a) 3–2
(Graydon 2, B. Little; 20,205)
Mar 15 Southampton (h) 3–0
(Leonard, Graydon, Holmes own goal; 31,967)
Mar 22 Orient (a) 0–1
(9,466)
Mar 29 West Brom (h) 3–1
(Leonard 2, Hamilton; 47,574)
Apr 1 Millwall (a) 3–1
(Hamilton, Leonard, B. Little; 13,115)
Apr 9 Cardiff (h) 2–0
(B. Little 2; 32,748)
Apr 12 Oldham (h) 5–0
(B. Little 3, Hicks own goal, Hamilton; 36,224)
Apr 19 Blackpool (a) 3–0
(Phillips, Hatton own goal, B. Little; 20,762)
Apr 23 Sheff Wed (a) 4–0
(Leonard, B. Little 2, Ross; 23,605)
Apr 26 Sunderland (h) 2–0
(Ross, B. Little; 57,266)
Apr 30 Norwich (a) 4–1
(Leonard, Gidman, McDonald, Carrodus; 35,999)

Final League Record

P	W	D	L	F	A	Pts	Pos
42	25	8	9	79	32	58	2nd

Football League Goalscorers: B. Little 20, Graydon 19, Hamilton 10, Leonard 7, Morgan 4, Nicholl 4, Carrodus 3, Phillips 2, Ross 2, Robson 1, Aitken 1, McDonald 1, Gidman 1, opp own goals 4.

FA Cup

Jan 4 (Rnd 3) Oldham (a) 3–0
(B. Little, Nicholl, Graydon; 14,510)
Jan 25 (Rnd 4) Sheff Utd (h) 4–1
(Leonard 2, Nicholl, Graydon; 35,881)
Feb 15 (Rnd 5) Ipswich (a) 2–3
(McDonald, Evans; 31,297)
FA Cup Goalscorers: Graydon 2, Leonard 2, Nicholl 2, B. Little, McDonald, Evans.

third round, tiny Crewe provided the shock by drawing 2–2 at Gresty Road and losing only 1–0 at Villa Park, and although Hartlepool managed a draw on their home ground, when they came to Aston they were smashed 6–1 for their pains. A 2–1 win at Colchester brought Villa an unattractive semi-final with Chester and in the first leg at Sealand Road, Villa twice took the lead, only to lose it in a 2–2 draw. Chester fought hard at Villa Park and Villa squeezed through 3–2 to ensure that Ron Saunders completed a unique hat-trick in taking three different clubs to the League Cup final in successive seasons.

It was also third time lucky for Saunders. Against his old club, Norwich, Ray Graydon scored from a rebound after City's Kevin Keelan had saved the Villa man's penalty kick. It was the only goal of a mediocre final and came a few minutes from the end. Nevertheless it put the icing on the cake for Aston Villa as they went on to clinch promotion. Villa were back again!

Football League Cup

Sep 11	(Rnd 2) Everton	(h)	1–1	
(Nicholl; 29,640)				
Sep 18	(Replay) Everton	(a)	3–0	
(Morgan, Carrodus, Graydon; 24,595)				
Oct 9	(Rnd 3) Crewe	(a)	2–2	
(Morgan, Leonard; 12,290)				
Oct 16	(Replay) Crewe	(h)	1–0	
(Hamilton; 24,007)				
Nov 12	(Rnd 4) Hartlepool	(a)	1–1	
(Aitken; 12,305)				
Nov 25	(Replay) Hartlepool	(h)	6–1	
(Hamilton 2, B. Little 2, Graydon 2; 17,686)				
Dec 3	(Rnd 5) Colchester	(a)	2–1	
(A. Little, Graydon; 11,871)				
Jan 15	(SF 1st leg) Chester	(a)	2–2	
(McDonald, Graydon; 19,000)				
Jan 22	(SF 2nd leg) Chester	(h)	3–2	
(Leonard 2, B. Little; 47,632)				
Mar 1	(Final) Norwich (Wembley)		1–0	
(Graydon; 100,000)				

Football League Cup Goalscorers: Graydon 6, B. Little 3, Hamilton 3, Leonard 3, Morgan 2, Nichol 1, McDonald 1, Carrodud 1, Aitken 1, A. Little 1.

We did it! Villa players celebrate their victory.

1975-6

Not only had Aston Villa brought First Division football back to their palatial stadium, they had also given Villa fans an entirely new experience in 1975-6 — European football. Since Manchester United took the first steps in 1956, English clubs had counted European competition as part and parcel of the everyday programme. Yet Villa, this most famous of clubs and the side which had pioneered much of football's early history, had never played a competitive European game at first team level. Now, as Football League Cup holders, they were entitled to a place in the UEFA Cup.

Unfortunately, Villa's first assualt on the bastions of Continental football came to an abrupt end almost before it had started. On 17 September 1975, Aston Villa took the field against Antwerp of Belgium with this side — the first to represent Villa in European competition — Cumbes; Gidman, Aitken, Ross, Nicholl, Phillips, Graydon, McDonald, Morgan, Hamilton and Carrodus. Robson substituted for McDonald during the match and Hamilton was

eventually replaced by Hunt. Almost at once, Villa found that this was a different game and a hat-trick by Kodat and a further goal by Heyligen, gave Antwerp a 4–1 win. At Villa Park on the first day of October, Villa tried to pull back that three-goal lead but Kodat scored again to increase the Belgians' advantage and Villa were dumped out 5–1 on aggregate. It was an inauspicious start to Villa's newfound status.

But the First Division was the most important thing to occupy Villa's attention and immediately after that European exit they drew 0–0 at Middlesbrough to go to eighth place in the table and set the fans thinking about a possible Championship. Before long, they would be thinking instead about a quick return to the Second Division, however. A succession of mediocre results put Villa into a midtable position by Christmas and as the season wore on they found themselves stuck in eighteenth place for the period between mid-March and mid-April. In the last three games of the season Villa

Manchester United's Martin Buchan (number 6) cannot prevent Andy Gray from rifling Villa's winning goal to give them their first win of 1976.

First Division results 1975-6

Aug 16 Leeds   (h)   2–1
(Phillips; 46,026)

Aug 19 QPR   (a)   1–1
(Leonard; 21,986)

Aug 23 Norwich   (a)   3–5
(Graydon 2, Aitken; 21,797)

Aug 27 Man City   (h)   1–0
(Leonard; 35,212)

Aug 30 Coventry   (h)   1–0
(Graydon; 41,026)

Sep 6 Newcastle   (a)   0–3
(34,668)

Sep 13 Arsenal   (h)   2–0
(Phillips, Leonard; 34,474)

Sep 20 Liverpool   (a)   0–3
(42,779)

Sep 23 Wolves   (a)   0–0
(33,344)

Sep 27 Birmingham   (h)   2–1
(Hamilton, Little; 53,782)

Oct 4 Middlesborough   (a)   0–0
(24,102)

Oct 11 Tottenham   (h)   1–1
(Gray; 40,048)

Oct 18 Everton   (a)   1–2
(Nicholl; 30,376)

Oct 25 Burnley   (h)   1–1
(Noble own goal; 34,242)

Nov 1 Ipswich   (a)   0–3
(24,691)

Nov 8 Sheff Utd   (h)   5–1
(Gray, Hamilton 2, Deehan, Graydon; 30,053)

Nov 15 Man United   (a)   0–2
(51,682)

Nov 22 Everton   (h)   3–1
(Gray 2, McNaught own goal; 33,949)

Nov 29 Leicester   (h)   1–1
(Graydon; 36,388)

Dec 6 Stoke   (a)   1–1
(Graydon; 28,492)

Dec 13 Norwich   (h)   3–2
(Graydon, Deehan 2; 30,478)

Dec 20 Leeds   (a)   0–1
(29,118)

Dec 26 West Ham   (h)   4–1
(Deehan 2, Hamilton, Gray; 51,300)

Dec 27 Derby   (a)   0–2
(37,230)

Jan 10 Arsenal   (a)   0–0
(24,501)

Jan 17 Newcastle   (h)   1–1
(McMahony own goal; 36,387)

Jan 31 QPR   (h)   0–2
(32,223)

Feb 7 Man City   (a)   1–2
(Gray; 32,331)

Feb 14 Sheff United   (a)   1–2
(Graydon; 21,152)

Feb 21 Man United   (h)   2–1
(McDonald, Gray; 50,094)

Feb 24 Wolves   (h)   1–1
(Graydon; 47,693)

Feb 28 Burnley   (a)   2–2
(Graydon, Gray; 17,123)

Mar 6 Ipswich   (h)   0–0
(32,477)

Mar 13 Tottenham   (a)   2–5
(Graydon, Gray; 23,169)

Mar 20 Leicester   (a)   2–2
(Nicholl 2; 24,663)

Mar 27 Stoke   (h)   0–0
(32,359)

Apr 3 Birmingham   (a)   2–3
(Gray, Graydon; 46,251)

Apr 10 Liverpool   (h)   0–0
(44,250)

Apr 13 Coventry   (a)   1–1
(Nicholl; 27,586)

Apr 17 West Ham   (a)   2–2
(Deehan, Hunt; 21,642)

Apr 19 Derby   (h)   1–0
(McDonald; 39,241)

Apr 24 Middlesbrough   (h)   2–1
(Deehan, Carrodus; 33,241)

Final League Record

P	W	D	L	F	A	Pts	Pos
42	11	17	14	51	59	39	16th

Football League Goalscorers: Graydon 12, Gray 10, Deehan 7, Nicholl 4, Hamilton 4, Leonard 3, Phillips 2, McDonald 2, Aitken 1, Little 1, Hunt 1, Carrodus 1, opp own goals 3.

FA Cup

Jan 3 (Rnd 3) Southampton   (a)   1–1
(Gray; 24,138)

Jan 7 (Replay) Southampton   (h)   1–2
(Graydon; 44,623)

FA Cup Goalscorers: Gray, Graydon.

Football League Cup

Sep 10 (Rnd 2) Oldham   (h)   2–0
(Leonard, Nicholl; 23,041)

Oct 8 (Rnd 3) Man United   (h)   1–2
(Gray; 41,447)

Football League Cup Goalscorers: Leonard, Gray, Nicholl.

UEFA Cup

Sep 17 (Rnd 1, 1st leg) Antwerp (a) 1–4
(Graydon; 20,000)
Oct 1 (1st Rnd, 2nd leg) Antwerp (h) 0–1
(31,513)
UEFA Cup Goalscorer: Graydon.

picked up five points with wins over Derby and Middlesbrough and a draw at West Ham and those vital points gave them a final position of sixteenth place. Even with three-up-and-three-down, Villa had avoided relegation by nine points as their neighbours Wolves joined Burnley and Sheffield United in the drop.

In the FA Cup, Southampton had won a third round replay at Villa Park when McCalliog had scored twice, although the game went to extra-time; in the Football League Cup, Macari and Coppell gave Manchester United a 2–1 win at Villa Park in the third round. All in all, the season had been an extremely disappointing one from the fans' point of view, although Saunders knew that he had at least settled the side down into the First Division.

Villa's £110,000 striker Andy Gray (out of picture) heads a debut goal past Alex Stepney. But Manchester United won this League Cup 3rd Round match 2-1.

1976-7

What a tremendous season this was for Aston Villa! Winners of the Football League Cup, never out of the top dozen placings in the First Division to finally finish in fourth place and so doubly qualify for the UEFA Cup, and also quarter-finalists in the FA Cup. The days of wine and roses and returned to Villa Park with a vengeance.

Villa started off the season with a resounding 4–0 win over West Ham United at Villa Park; they finished it with an equally emphatic 4–0 win over West Bromwich Albion, also at Villa Park, and in between sandwiched all sorts of goodies for their diehard fans. Although they ultimately failed to finish in the first three in the First Division, Villa were up at the top for a long time. After beating Arsenal 5–1 at Villa Park on 20 October, they moved into second place and until they drew 0–0 at Bristol City on 2 April, they were never out of the top five.

Former Dundee United striker Andy Gray hit twenty-five of Villa's seventy-six League goals and in defence goalkeeper John Burridge and defenders John Gidman, Gordon Smith, Leighton Phillips, Chris Nicholl and Dennis Mortimer kept a tight rein on opposition attacks, conceding just fifty goals in Villa's forty-two League matches. Undoubtedly Villa's best win of the season was their 5–1 victory over the champions Liverpool on 15 December.

In the FA Cup, Villa reached the last eight before Manchester United beat them 2–1 in the seething cauldron of Old Trafford; the Football League Cup provided Villa with their main reason for celebration in 1976-7. Right from the start of the League Cup campaign Villa looked as though they were determined to win the trophy. They whipped Manchester City 3–0, beat Norwich 2–1, had another big win over Wrexham who they thrashed

How the national press saw the riot between rival fans during Villa's match with Glasgow Rangers on October 9th 1976.

First Division results 1976-7

Aug 21 West Ham (h) 4–0
(Gray 2, Graydon 2; 39,012)

Aug 25 Man City (a) 0–2
(41,007)

Aug 28 Everton (a) 2–0
(Little, Lyons own goal; 32,058)

Sep 4 Ipswich (h) 5–2
(Little, Gray 3, Graydon; 39,916)

Sep 11 QPR (a) 1–2
(Gray; 23,602)

Sep 18 Birmingham (h) 1–2
(Gray; 50,084)

Sep 25 Leicester (h) 2–0
(Graydon, Gray; 36,652)

Oct 2 Stoke (a) 0–1
(29,652)

Oct 16 Sunderland (a) 1–0
(Cropley; 31,578)

Oct 20 Arsenal (h) 5–1
(Mortimer, Graydon, Gray 2, Little; 33,860)

Oct 23 Bristol City (h) 3–1
(Nicholl, Gidman, Graydon; 37,094)

Oct 30 Liverpool (a) 0–3
(51,751)

Nov 6 Man United (h) 3–2
(Mortimer, Gray 2; 44,789)

Nov 10 West Brom (a) 1–1
(Mortimer; 42,900)

Nov 20 Coventry (h) 2–2
(Gidman, Gray; 40,047)

Nov 27 Norwich (a) 1–1
(Little; 22,554)

Dec 11 Leeds (a) 3–1
(Gray 2, Cropley; 31,232)

Dec 15 Liverpool (h) 5–1
(Gray 2, Deehan, Little; 42,851)

Dec 18 Newcastle (h) 2–1
(Deehan 2; 33,982)

Dec 27 Middlesbrough (a) 2–3
(Gray, Hughes; 31,000)

Jan 1 Man United (a) 0–2
(55,446)

Jan 22 West Ham (a) 1–0
(Gray; 27,577)

Feb 5 Everton (h) 2–0
(Gray, Little; 41,305)

Feb 12 Ipswich (a) 0–1
(29,750)

Mar 2 Derby (h) 4–0
(Mortimer, Gidman, Little, Cowans; 37,396)

Mar 5 Leicester (a) 1–1
(Deehan; 22,038)

Mar 23 Sunderland (h) 4–1
(Gidman, Gray, Deehan 2; 34,458)

Apr 2 Bristol City (a) 0–0
(27,958)

Apr 5 Middlesbrough (h) 1–0
(Deehan; 32,646)

Apr 9 Derby (a) 1–2
(Little; 28,061)

Apr 16 Coventry (a) 3–2
(Cowans, Deehan, Little; 31,158)

Apr 20 Tottenham (h) 2–1
(Little, Deehan; 42,047)

Apr 23 Norwich (h) 1–0
(Little; 35,899)

Apr 25 Arsenal (a) 0–3
(23,961)

Apr 30 Tottenham (a) 1–3
(Deehan; 30,890)

May 4 Man City (h) 1–1
(Little; 36,190)

May 7 Leeds Utd (h) 2–1
(Deehan, Cropley; 38,205)

May 10 Birmingham (a) 1–2
(Deehan; 43,721)

May 14 Newcastle (a) 2–3
(Little 2; 29,250)

May 16 Stoke (h) 1–0
(Gray; 28,963)

May 20 QPR (h) 1–1
(Cowans; 28,056)

May 23 West Brom (h) 4–0
(Nicholl, Gray 3; 42,542)

Final League Record

P	W	D	L	F	A	Pts	Pos
42	22	7	13	76	50	51	4th

Football League goalscorers: Gray 25, Little 14, Deehan 13, Graydon 6, Mortimer 4, Gidman 4, Cowans 3, Cropley 3, Nicholl 2, Hughes 1, Opp own goal 1.

FA Cup

Jan 8 (Rnd 3) Leicester (a) 1–0
(Gray; 27,112)

Jan 29 (Rnd 4) West Ham (h) 3–0
(Deehan 2, Mortimer; 46,954)

Feb 26 (Rnd 5) Port Vale (h) 3–0
(Nicholl, Little, Deehan; 46,872)

Mar 19 (Rnd 6) Man Utd (a) 1–2
(Little; 57,089)

F.A. Cup Goalscorers: Deehan 3, Little 2, Gray 1, Mortimer 1, Nicholl 1.

5–1, and removed Millwall 2–0 to reach the semifinal against QPR. Rangers spent £12,000 on a system of hot air balloons to dry out Loftus Road sufficiently for the first-leg to be played. The result was a 0–0 draw. At Villa Park, Gerry Francis sent the game into extra-time at 1–1. There were further thrills as Deehan shot Villa in front again, Burridge saved a penalty, and then QPR substitute Eastoe made it 2–2 in the 115th minute of the game. At Highbury six days later, the sides tried again and this time Brian Little scored a hat-trick as Villa romped home 3–0.

It took three games with Everton in the final before Villa finally lifted the League Cup. The Wembley game ended 0–0 with no extra-time played; and the Hillsborough replay was a 1–1 draw, this time after extra-time. It was almost a month before the game was replayed for a second time — this one at Old Trafford — Latchford scored first for Everton, and three goals in four minutes near the end — Nicholl and Little for Villa and Lyons for Everton — made extra-time look a certainty until Little scored the winner with less than a minute to play. Over 210,000 people had watched the three games. And Villa were back in Europe for the second time.

The League Cup final second replay at Hillsborough which ended 1–1. Everton goalkeeper Dave Lawson punches clear from Villa's Chris Nicholl.

Football League Cup

Sep 1	(Rnd 2)	Man City	(h)	3–0
(Little 2, Graydon; 34,585)				
Sep 21	(Rnd 3)	Norwich	(h)	2–1
(Gray 2; 31,295)				
Oct 27	(Rnd 4)	Wrexham	(h)	5–1
(Little 2, Nicholl, Carrodus, Gray; 41,428)				
Dec 1	(Rnd 5)	Millwall	(h)	2–0
(Nicholl, Little; 37,147)				
Feb 1	(SF 1st leg)	QPR	(a)	0–0
(28,739)				
Feb 16	(SF 2nd leg)	QPR	(h)	2–2
(Deehan 2; 48,439)				
Feb 22	(Replay)	QPR	(n)	3–0
(Little 3; 40,438)				
Mar 12	(Final)	Everton (Wembley)		0–0
(100,000)				
Mar 16	(Replay)	Everton (Hillsbro)		1–1
(Kenyon own goal; 55,000)				
Apr 13	(Replay)	Everton (Old Traff)		3–2
(Little 2, Nicholl; 54,749)				

Football League Cup Goalscorers: Little 10, Nicholl 3, Gray 3, Deehan 2, Graydon, Carrodus, opp own goal 1.

1977-8

Villa did much better in their second attempt at a European trophy and they reached the quarter-finals of the UEFA Cup with some good wins over some of the more famous names in European soccer. In the First Division, too, they did well, although finishing in eighth place and never striking the highs spots of the previous season. In fact, eighth place was the highest position that the club managed in the table all season and they finally achieved it with a fine 6-1 win over Ipswich Town in the penultimate game of the season, and maintained it despite a disappointing 3-1 defeat at Molineux on the last day. Again, Andy Gray was leading scorer with thirteen goals and in goal the former Manchester United, Swansea and Arsenal goalkeeper Jimmy Rimmer played in every match.

The domestic cups were a disappointment. In the Football League Cup, Villa reached the fourth round via Exeter and QPR, before Brian Clough's Nottingham Forest beat them 4-2 at the City Ground. Villa's FA Cup run ended even earlier when Everton gained some crumb of revenge for

Euro action. John Deehan heads Villa 2-0 ahead against Turkish side Fenerbahce in the UEFA Cup.

their League Cup final defeat by Villa, when they won 4-1 at Goodison Park in the third round.

In the UEFA Cup, Villa did much better. Their first round match was against the Hungarian team, Fenerbache, and after Deehan (2), Gray and Little gave Villa a 4-0 start at Villa Park, they had little trouble in adding a further two goals in Hungary. The first-leg of the second round was also played at Villa Park and this time the Poles of Gornik Zabrze gave away a two-goal deficit and were unable to pull it back in Poland. So to the third round and the Spaniards, Atletico Bilbao, the side which had once had an epic struggle with Manchester United in the early days of the European Cup. Again Villa were at home first and again they won 2-0. Yet again they managed a 1-1 draw in the Basque port and Villa fans looked forward eagerly to another home first-leg, this time against Spanish football's other representatives, CF Barcelona.

At this point, Villa were unable to gain the lead. In fact Barcelona took a 2-0 lead through Cruyff, the Dutch master, and Zuvira. In the eighty-second minute Cruyff limped off to an ovation from the Villa crowd and in the last four minutes Villa drew

First Division results 1977-8

Agu 20   QPR   (a)   2-1
(Deehan, Carrodus; 25,431)

Aug 24   Man City   (h)   1-4
(Deehan; 40,121)

Aug 27   Everton   (h)   1-2
(Gray; 37,806)

Sep 3   Bristol City   (a)   1-1
(Little; 20,200)

Sep 10   Arsenal   (h)   1-0
(Cropley; 36,929)

Sep 17   Nottm Forest   (a)   0-2
(31,016)

Sep 23   Wolves   (h)   2-0
(Brazier own goal, Deehan; 40,403)

Oct 1   Birmingham   (h)   0-1
(45,436)

Oct 5   Leeds   (a)   1-1
(Gray; 27,797)

Oct 8   Leicester   (a)   2-0
(Cowans, Gray; 20,276)

Oct 15   Norwich   (h)   3-0
(Gray, Cowans, Little; 32,978)

Oct 22   West Ham   (a)   2-2
(McNaught, Gray; 26,599)

Oct 29   Man United   (h)   2-1
(Gray, Cropley; 39,144)

Nov 5   Liverpool   (a)   2-1
(Gray 2; 50,436)

Nov 12   Middlesbrough   (h)   0-1
(31,837)

Nov 19   Chelsea   (a)   0-0
(31,764)

Dec 3   Ipswich   (a)   0-2
(20,917)

Dec 10   West Brom   (h)   3-0
(Cowans, Gray, Gidman; 41,631)

Dec 17   Middlesbrough   (a)   0-1
(14,999)

Dec 26   Coventry   (h)   1-1
(Deehan; 43,571)

Dec 27   Derby   (a)   3-0
(Little, Gray, Deehan; 30,395)

Dec 31   Man City   (a)   0-2
(46,074)

Jan 2   QPR   (h)   1-1
(Little; 34,750)

Jan 14   Everton   (a)   0-1
(40,630)

Jan 28   Bristol City   (h)   1-0
(Deehan; 29,676)

Feb 4   Arsenal   (a)   1-0
(McDonald own goal; 30,127)

Feb 25   Birmingham   (a)   0-1
(33,679)

Mar 4   Leicester   (h)   0-0
(29,971)

Mar 11   Norwich   (a)   1-2
(Gregory; 19,031)

Mar 18   West Ham   (h)   4-1
(Gregory 2, Deehan, Mortimer; 28,275)

Mar 21   Coventry   (a)   3-2
(Little, McNaught, Gray; 30,957)

Mar 25   Derby   (h)   0-0
(32,793)

Mar 29   Man United   (a)   1-1
(Deehan; 41,625)

Apr 1   Liverpool   (h)   0-3
(40,190)

Apr 5   Nottm Forest   (h)   0-1
(44,215)

Apr 8   Newcastle   (a)   1-1
(Evans; 17,203)

Apr 15   Chelsea   (h)   2-0
(Cowans, Wicks own goal; 27,375)

Apr 17   Newcastle   (h)   2-0
(Cowans, Gray; 25,493)

Apr 22   West Brom   (a)   3-0
(Deehan, Cowans, Mortimer; 35,000)

Apr 26   Leeds   (h)   3-1
(Deehan, Mortimer, Little; 30,524)

Apr 29   Ipswich   (h)   6-1
(Deehan 2, Gray, Little, Carrodus, Cowans; 30,955)

May 2   Wolves   (a)   1-3
(Carrodus; 30,644)

Final League Record

P	W	D	L	F	A	Pts	Pos
42	18	10	14	57	42	46	8th

Football League Goalscorers: Gray 13, Deehan 12, Little 7, Cowans 7, Carrodus 3, Gregory 3, Mortimer 3, Cropley 2, McNaught 2, Gidman 1, Evans 1, opp own goals 3.

FA Cup

Jan 7   (Rnd 3) Everton   (a)   1-4
(Gray; 46,320)

FA Cup Goalscorer: Gray.

Football League Cup

Aug 31   (Rnd 2) Exeter   (a)   3-1
(Gray 3; 13,768)

Oct 26   (Rnd 3) QPR   (h)   1-0
(Gray; 34,481)

Nov 29   (Rnd 4) Nottm Forest   (a)   2-4
(Little, Caradus; 29,333)

Football League Cup Goalscorers: Gray 4, Little, Carrodus)

UEFA Cup

Sep 14 (Rnd 1, 1st leg) Fenerbahce (h) 4–0
(Gray, Deehan 2, Little; 30,351)
Sep 28 (Rnd 1, 2nd leg) Fenerbahce (a) 2–0
(Deehan, Little; 25,000)
Oct 19 (Rnd 2, 1st leg) Gornick Z (h) 2–0
(McNaught 2; 34,138)
Nov 2 (Rnd 2, 2nd leg) Gornik Z (a) 1–1
(Gray; 15,000)
Nov 23 (Rnd 3, 1st leg) Ath Bilbao (h) 2–0
(Iribar own goal, Deehan; 32,973)
Dec 12 (Rnd 3, 2nd leg) Ath Bilbao (a) 1–1
(Mortimer; 39,000)
Mar 1 (QF 1st leg) Barcelona (h) 2–2
(McNaught, Deehan; 49,619)
Mar 15 (QF 2nd leg) Barcelona (a) 1–2
(Little; 90,000)
Aston Villa lost 3–4 on aggregate.
UEFA Cup Goalscorers: Deehan 5, Little 3, McNaught 3, Gray 2, Mortimer 1, opp own goal 1.

level when McNaught and Deehan staged a grandstand finish. In Barcelona's wondrous stadium Villa might have won had not John Gidman been sent off in the twenty-third minute. Even then they took the lead through Little, but the strain of playing with ten men soon told and Migueli and Asensi scored the goals which put Barcelona into the hat for the semi-final draw.

Deehan celebrates again — but this 'goal' against Bilbao in the UEFA Cup was disallowed.

1978-9

Aston Villa again finished eighth in the First Division to establish themselves as one of English football's better and more consistent sides. Nevertheless, this was a mediocre season in many ways, remembered as much as anything for Villa's short but eventful League Cup run which ended in the fourth round, but which involved five matches and some unpleasant incidents.

Villa's Football League Cup first round match against Sheffield United at Villa Park towards the end of August was uneventful enough and young Gary Shelton gave them a 1-0 win. But there then followed three bruising encounters with Crystal Palace. The first match at Villa Park on 4 October saw Villa draw 1-1 and Shelton was carried off with an unpleasant leg injury. Manager Ron Saunders declared angrily after the match: 'I keep reading about these sides that want to come and play football; but all that happens is that they want to try and kick you off the pitch.' In the replay at Selhurst Park, Villa and Palace made a 0-0 draw and Villa defender Allan Evans was sent off. At the third attempt, Villa won 3-0 with goals from Gray (2) and Gregory and at last Luton Town knew who they would be facing in the next round. It was Luton who gave football a shock when they won 2-0 at Villa Park to knock out the club which had done so well in the League Cup. Villa had Gray carried off and never recovered.

Villa also had no reason to remember the FA Cup of 1978-9. In the third round they went to the City Ground, Nottingham, where Forest beat them 2-0 and John Deehan was sent off in another futile incident which cost Villa dearly.

In the First Division, Jimmy Rimmer played another full season as Villa coasted to a respectable place behind the leaders. Full-back John Robson had his contract cancelled in November after it was learned that he was suffering from multiple sclerosis in one of the most tragic blows suffered by a professional player in recent years. Villa staged a testimonial match for Robson later on, but it was a sad blow, both to the club and to a very fine player. Robson had made 144 League appearances for Villa (three as a substitute) to add to the 171 (plus one as substitute) he had made for Derby County. Villa ended the season on an indifferent note when they lost two of their last three games, ending up with a 3-2 win over Manchester City at Maine Road. Ron Saunders was to suffer, like his predecessors, the slings and arrows of boardroom battles at Villa Park. It is a tribute to his ability, dignity and professionalism, that, above all, he has carried on trying to give Villa supporters the team which they deserve.

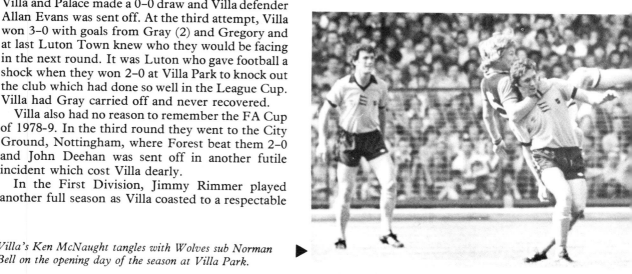

Villa's Ken McNaught tangles with Wolves sub Norman Bell on the opening day of the season at Villa Park.

Forest's Peter Shilton punches off the head of John Deehan in the FA Cup 3rd round tie between the two clubs. Forest won 2-0.

First Division results 1978-9

Aug 19 Wolves (h) 1–0
(Gray; 43,922)

Aug 23 Tottenham (a) 4–1
(A. Evans, Gregory, Little, Shelton; 47,892)

Aug 26 Bristol City (a) 0–1
(23,493)

Sep 2 Southampton (h) 1–1
(Gray; 34,067)

Sep 9 Ipswich (a) 2–0
(Gregory, Gray; 22,166)

Sep 16 Everton (h) 1–1
(Craig; 38,636)

Sep 23 QPR (a) 0–1
(16,410)

Sep 30 Nottm Forest (h) 1–2
(Craig pen; 36,735)

Oct 7 Arsenal (a) 1–1
(Gregory; 34,537)

Oct 14 Man United (h) 2–2
(Gregory 2; 36,204)

Oct 21 Birmingham (a) 1–0
(Gray; 36,145)

Oct 27 Middlesbrough (h) 0–2
(32,615)

Nov 4 Man City (h) 1–1
(Deehan; 32,724)

Nov 11 Wolves (a) 4–0
(Shelton, McNaught, Deehan, Mortimer; 23,289)

Nov 18 Bristol City (h) 2–0
(Deehan, Cowans; 27,621)

Nov 21 Southampton (a) 0–2
(20,880)

Nov 25 West Brom (a) 1–1
(A. Evans; 35,085)

Dec 9 Chelsea (a) 1–0
(A. Evans; 19,080)

Dec 16 Norwich (h) 1–1
(McQuire own goal; 26,228)

Dec 23 Derby (a) 0–0
(20,109)

Dec 26 Leeds (h) 2–2
(Gregory 2; 40,973)

Jan 31 Everton (a) 1–1
(Shelton; 29,079)

Feb 24 Man United (a) 1–1
(Albiston own goal; 44,473)

Mar 3 Birmingham (h) 1–0
(Cowans; 42,419)

Mar 7 Bolton (h) 3–0
(Gray, Swain, Jones own goal; 28,053)

Mar 10 Middlesbrough (a) 0–2
(16,562)

Mar 20 QPR (h) 3–1
(A. Evans, Gidman pen, Mortimer; 24,310)

Mar 24 Tottenham (h) 2–3
(Gidman pen, Gray; 35,486)

Mar 28 Coventry (h) 1–1
(A. Evans; 25,670)

Apr 4 Nottm Forest (a) 0–4
(27,056)

Apr 7 Coventry (a) 1–1
(Deehan; 23,690)

Apr 11 Derby (h) 3–3
(Cowans 2, Gidman pen; 21,884)

Apr 14 Leeds (a) 0–1
(24,281)

Apr 16 Liverpool (h) 3–1
(A. Evans, Thompson own goal, Deehan; 44,029)

Apr 21 Norwich (a) 2–1
(Shelton, Cropley; 15,061)

Apr 25 Arsenal (h) 5–1
(Shelton 3 (1 pen), Deehan 2; 26,168)

Apr 28 Chelsea (h) 2–1
(G. Wilkins own goal, Deehan; 29,219)

May 2 Ipswich (h) 2–2
(Swain, Deehan; 26,636)

May 5 Bolton (a) 0–0
(17,394)

May 8 Liverpool (a) 0–3
(50,570)

May 11 West Brom (h) 0–1
(35,991)

May 15 Man City (a) 3–2
(Cropley, Mortimer, Deehan; 30,028)

Final League Record

P	W	D	L	F	A	Pts	Pos
42	15	16	11	59	49	46	8th

Football League Goalscorers: Deehan 10, Gregory 7, Shelton 7, Gray 6, A. Evans 6, Cowans 4, Mortimer 3, Gidman 3, Craig 2, Swain 2, Cropley 2, Little 1, McNaught 1, opp own goal 5.

FA Cup

Jan 10 (Rnd 3) Nottm Forest (a) 0–2
(29,550)

Football League Cup

Aug 30 (Rnd 2) Sheff Wed (h) 1–0
(Shelton; 31,152)

Oct 4 (Rnd3) Crystal P (h) 1–1
(Little; 30,690)

Oct 10 (Replay) Crystal P (a) 0–0
(33,155)

Oct 16 (Replay) Crystal P (n) 3–0
(Gray 2, Gregory; 25,445)

Nov 8 (Rnd 4) Luton (h) 0–2
(32,737)

Football League Cup Goalscorers: Gray 2, Shelton, Little, Gregory.

1979-80

Aston Villa fans can look back on the 1979-80 season with great satisfaction. Although their famous club did not take any major honours, Villa finished high in the First Division and reached the quarter-finals of the FA Cup before going out to the eventual finalists West Ham United.

Villa's season started quietly enough with a 1-1 draw against doomed-to-be-relegated Bolton Wanderers at Burnden Park. They finished it on the last Saturday of the season with a 4-1 hiding at Anfield where Liverpool clinched the championship which they had been threatening to take all season. But in between there were some high spots for Aston Villa in the Cup, although it has to be said that Villa's progress to the last eight was at the expense of several lowly teams. In fact Villa did not play a First Division side in the FA Cup.

The club's first cup challenge came in late August when they beat Colchester United 2-0 at Layer Road in the second round first-leg of the Football League Cup. It was a result which gave Villa confidence for the return at Villa Park but it was United who did all

the running before reversing the scoreline and leaving Villa severely embarrassed before they scraped through on penalty kicks. In the next round Everton managed a goalless draw at Villa Park and in the replay it was obvious from early on that Villa had missed their chance. The Merseysiders won 4-1 with Swain getting the lone Villa goal.

In the FA Cup things went better for Villa. After removing Bristol Rovers 2-1 at Eastville in the third round they faced a difficult away game against Second Division Cambridge United and the relative newcomers to the Football League managed a 1-1 draw before sliding 4-1 at Villa Park, although as one United supporter commented: 'It was enough to see United run out at such a famous ground when not so long ago we were in the Southern League.' Third Division title hopefuls Blackburn Rovers also proved difficult to dislodge, drawing 1-1 at Ewood Park before Evans squeezed Villa through at Aston.

Jimmy Rimmer blocks an Everton shot at Villa Park. Villa won 2-1 to continue their fine run in the First Division.

First Division results 1979-80

Aug 18   Bolton   (a)   1-1
(Cowans; 19,795)

Aug 22   Brighton   (h)   2-1
(Evans, Morley; 28,803)

Aug 25   Bristol City   (h)   0-2
(25,526)

Sep 1   Everton   (a)   1-1
(Morley; 29,271)

Sep 8   Man United   (h)   0-3
(34,859)

Sep 15   Crystal Palace   (a)   0-2
(28,156)

Sep 22   Arsenal   (h)   0-0
(27,277)

Sep 29   Middlesbrough   (a)   0-0
(16,017)

Oct 6   Southampton   (h)   3-0
(Bremner, Mortimer, Evans; 24,377)

Oct 13   West Brom   (h)   0-0
(36,007)

Oct 20   Derby   (a)   3-1
(Little, Shaw, Mortimer; 20,152)

Oct 27   Wolves   (a)   1-1
(Shaw; 36,262)

Nov 3   Bolton   (h)   3-1
(Shaw, Evans, Mortimer; 24,744)

Nov 10   Ipswich   (a)   0-0
(17,807)

Nov 17   Stoke   (h)   2-1
(Mortimer, Evans; 27,086)

Nov 24   Leeds   (h)   0-0
(29,736)

Dec 1   Norwich   (a)   1-1
(Evans; 15,885)

Dec 8   Liverpool   (h)   1-3
(Little; 41,160)

Dec 15   Tottenham   (a)   2-1
(Geddis, Cowans; 30,555)

Dec 19   Coventry   (h)   3-0
(Donovan, Little 2; 24,446)

Dec 26   Nottm Forest   (a)   1-2
(Shaw; 30,979)

Dec 29   Bristol City   (a)   3-1
(Shaw 3; 18,221)

Jan 12   Everton   (h)   2-1
(Gibson, Donovan; 31,108)

Feb 2   Crystal Palace   (h)   2-0
(Cowans, Mortimer; 29,469)

Feb 9   Arsenal   (a)   1-3
(Mortimer; 33,816)

Feb 23   West Brom   (a)   2-1
(McNaught, Little; 33,658)

Feb 27   Man City   (h)   2-2
(Shaw, opp own goal; 29,139)

Mar 1   Derby   (h)   1-0
(Evans; 28,596)

Mar 3   Brighton   (a)   1-1
(Evans; 23,077)

Mar 10   Wolves   (h)   1-3
(Shaw; 30,432)

Mar 15   Southampton   (a)   0-2
(20,735)

Mar 19   Middlesbrough   (h)   0-2
(15,319)

Mar 22   Ipswich   (h)   1-1
(Morley; 22,386)

Mar 26   Norwich   (h)   2-0
(Cowans, Hopkins; 17,956)

Mar 29   Stoke   (a)   0-2
(16,234)

Apr 5   Nottm Forest   (h)   3-2
(Bremner, Evans, opp own goal; 29,156)

Apr 7   Man City   (a)   1-1
(Geddis; 42,584)

Apr 19   Leeds   (a)   0-0
(15,840)

Apr 23   Man United   (a)   1-2
(Bremner; 45,201)

Apr 26   Tottenham   (h)   1-0
(Cowans; 29,549)

Apr 29   Coventry   (a)   2-1
(Gibson, Cowans; 17,969)

May 3   Liverpool   (a)   1-4
(opp own goal; 51,541)

Final League Record

P	W	D	L	F	A	Pts	Pos
42	16	14	12	51	50	46	7th

Football League Goalscorers: Shaw 9, Evans 8, Cowans 6, Mortimer 6, Little 5, Morley 3, Bremner 3, Geddis 2, Donovan 2, Gibson 2, Hopkins 1, McNaught 1, opp own goals 3

FA Cup

Jan 4   (Rnd 3) Bristol Rovers   (a)   2-1
(Shaw, Cowans; 16,060)

Jan 26   (Rnd 4) Cambridge U   (a)   1-1
(Donovan; 12,000)

Jan 30   (Replay) Cambridge U   (h)   4-1
(Donovan 2, Evans, Little; 36,835)

Feb 16   (Rnd 5) Blackburn   (a)   1-1
(Geddis; 29,468)

Feb 20   (Replay) Blackburn   (h)   1-0
(Evans; 42,161)

Mar 8   (Rnd 6) West Ham   (a)   0-1
(36,393)

FA Cup goalscorers: Donovan 3, Evans 2, Geddis, Little, Shaw, Cowans.

Football League Cup

Aug 28 (Rnd 2 1st leg) Colchester (a) 2-0
(Shaw 2; 6,221)
Sep 15 (Rnd 2 2nd leg) Colchester (h) 0-2
(19,473. Villa won on penalties)
Sep 25 (Rnd 3) Everton (h) 0-0
(22,635)
Oct 9 (Replay) Everton (a) 1-4
(Swain; 22,080)

Football League Cup Goalscorers: Shaw 2,
Swain.

And so to West Ham! Villa fans must have felt that this was their year for Wembley. Into the quarterfinal and without a First Division team played, they came up against Second Division Hammers with every reason to be making travelling arrangements to London on May 10. But it was not to be and the only bubbles being blown were by West Ham supporters as they saw their team win 1-0 at Upton Park and send Villa back up the M1 with their tails between their legs.

There was the usual boardroom battle in 1979-80 and the usual speculation that Brian Clough would be coming to take over, although as Clough reminded the sporting Press: 'Villa already have a manager — and a good one. I hope he's there for years!' The Eighties look to be particularly good times for Aston Villa Football Club. It's a long way from Aston Lower Meadow in terms of progress — and Villa can look forward to a decade of success if the signs are to be believed.

It's late in the season and Villa move up to fifth place in the First Division thanks to Gordon Cowan's winner against Coventry City at Highfield Road. Jim Blyth goes the right way but Cowan's penalty still beats him.

TWELVE GREAT VILLA PLAYERS

JAMES COWAN was the most outstanding centre-half in the game during the 1890s. An unknown with Vale of Leven reserves when he signed for Villa, he went on to play in three FA Cup Finals for the club and was the pivot of the magnificent half-back line of Reynolds, Cowan and Crabtree which took the 'Double' to Villa Park in 1897. Cowan earned his reputation with uncanny anticipation, a great tactical mind and a powerful tackle. He marshalled the Villa defence and was one of the great stars of his day, although he only won three Scottish international caps. Cowan was the man who won the famous Powderhall sprint under an assumed name — and was then fined and suspended by a furious Villa committee when they found out. Clearly he was one of the great characters of Victorian soccer.

'PONGO' WARING signed for Aston Villa in February 1928 and is still the holder of the club's individual scoring record for one season with his forty-nine goals in the 1930-1 First Division. Waring came to Villa Park from Tranmere Rovers and came to the attention of the bigger clubs after scoring six goals against Durham City in 1928. Liverpool wanted him but Tranmere dare not risk losing their supporters if Waring made the short trip to Anfield, and so Villa stepped in and got their man. In his first game in a Villa shirt — against Birmingham City Reserves — Waring scored a hat-trick and over 23,000 fans turned up see Villa's new star. He won five England caps while with Villa and was eventually transferred to Barnsley in 1935, returning to the Black Country with Wolves for a short while before finishing off his career where he began it at Tranmere.

FRANK BARSON was probably the toughest man ever to play professional football. An apprentice blacksmith when Barnsley signed him in 1911, he made himself 'known' on the Second Division pitches of pre-World War I. Barson's uncompromising tactics made him unpopular and after one cup-tie between Barnsley and Everton he had to be smuggled into a taxi outside Goodison Park. In October 1919 he signed for Villa for £2,850 and began to revitalise the team. That same season he won his only England cap against Wales at Highbury. Barson had many brushes with authority and was suspended several times. On Boxing Day 1921 he headed Villa's winning goal from 30yds against Sheffield United. It was to be his last season with the club and he was transferred to Manchester United, where he spent six seasons, and later played with Watford, Hartlepools and Wigan Borough before retiring in 1930-1

CLEM STEPHENSON joined Aston Villa from West Stanley in 1910 and although he played only once for his country (England v Wales in 1924) he was without doubt one of the greatest inside-forwards to play in the Football League between the wars. In 190 appearances for Villa between 1910 and 1921, Stephenson scored eighty-five goals; Villa sold him to Huddersfield Town, thinking him past his best, but Stephenson guided Huddersfield to three consecutive First Division Championships and played on until 1928-9. He won FA Cup-winners medals with Villa in 1913 and 1920. In that 1913 final, Stephenson told Sunderland's Charlie Buchan that he had dreamt that Villa would win 1–0 with a goal headed by Tommy Barber. They did!

ERIC HOUGHTON was a Lincolnshire lad from Billingborough and he skippered Donnington Grammar School near the tulip fields of Spalding. He signed for Aston Villa in August 1927 as a seventeenyear-old and played in the Villa side for two decades, scoring over 200 goals in all first team matches. Although he missed a penalty on his debut against Leeds United in January 1930, Houghton later converted fifty-eight spot kicks and also scored direct from about thirty free-kicks. When he played his very last game for Villa — in a Central League match against Huddersfield at the end of 1946 — he scored again — from the penalty spot. Houghton played seven times for England between 1931, when he made his debut against Northern Ireland, and 1933. He later became Villa's manager and later still, a director. He also played cricket with Lincolnshire and with Warwickshire Second Eleven.

ALEX MASSIE's second-ever game in an Aston Villa shirt was probably his most memorable — but for all the wrong reasons. For after signing for Villa from Hearts in December 1935 and making his debut against Manchester City, Massie found himself face to face with Arsenal at Villa Park. It was the day that Ted Drake cracked home all seven of Arsenal's goals — six with his first seven shots — and poor Aston Villa and their new wing-half were shattered. But Massie was to go on to help Villa to promotion after they had fallen from the First Division; and he also captained the side and played throughout the war which robbed him of so much of his first class career. Massie made a few appearances in the League South of 1945-6 and was eventually made team manager at Villa Park. He was a superb, ball-playing wing-half and won eighteen Scottish caps, seven of them with Villa.

HARRY PARKES was a great Villa servant — and a great practical joker. He played with GEC in Birmingham Works soccer and later with Boldmere St Michaels before signing for Villa as a young amateur in 1939. He played many times during wartime first team soccer and actually turned out in every position on the field, including goalkeeper when he was emergency replacement in a match with Wolves. He played many hundreds of games for Villa in their half-back line and was always good for a prank, although just occasionally his teammates caught *him* out. When he retired to look after his sports shop in 1955, Parkes had served Villa as well as any man and he later became a director of the club he loved so much.

TREVOR FORD was a fiery Welsh centre-forward who became a legend in his own playing lifetime. He was a native of Swansea and first played for his home town club, from where Villa bought him for £9,500 in January 1947. He stayed with the club until October 1950 and his spell at Villa Park brought fifty-nine goals in League games alone. He was eventually transferred to Sunderland for £30,000 and later saw service with Cardiff, PSV Eindhoven of Holland and Newport County where he finished his career in 1960-1. Ford's rugged style brought him a total of 177 goals in the grand total of 349 league games in which he played and he was always popular with his home crowds, although, strangely enough, less at Villa Park than some other clubs. He also gained thirty-eight caps for Wales.

Although **DANNY BLANCHFLOWER** enjoyed most of his success with Tottenham Hotspur, he was one of the greatest players ever to pull on the famous claret and blue shirt of Aston Villa. For almost five seasons, the style of Blanchflower graced Villa Park and his eventual departure was a significant day for the club. He first played with Northern Irish side Glentoran and then signed for Barnsley in 1948-9, eventually arriving at Villa Park in time to play eleven games of the 1950-1 season. He stayed with Villa until his move to Tottenham in 1954-5 and during that time played in 169 League games, scored ten goals, and won ten of his eventual fifty-six international caps. He left Villa because he thought the club was not ambitious enough and later events proved him right, although he would probably be proud of the steps the club has made since those dark days.

PETER McPARLAND suffers the misfortune to be constantly remembered as the man who put Ray Wood out of the 1957 FA Cup final with a shoulder charge which left the Manchester United goalkeeper with a fractured cheekbone. Yet McParland did what any forward was entitled to do in those days and there was certainly nothing malicious in his challenge. He did not let the incident put him off, however, and scored both Villa's goals as they won the cup. McParland signed for Villa as a youngster from Belfast and made his debut in 1952-3. He played his last game for the club in 1961-2 before going to Wolves and later to Plymouth and then America. He won thirty-four Northern Ireland caps and there can have been few more thrilling sights in the 1950s and 1960s, than McParland in full flight. He was a devastating match-winner who scored over 100 goals for Villa alone.

DEREK DOUGAN — 'The Doog' — joined Villa from Blackburn Rovers in the 1961 close season for £15,000 as a badly-needed replacement for Gerry Hitchens. Dougan played in the Football League Cup Final against Rotherham United in September 1961 — the game was held over from the previous season — but then sustained injuries in a car accident that ruled him out of the Villa side for some time. Dougan was always a controversial player and a short while after joining Villa he shaved his head to the astonishment of his teammates and Villa Park fans. His stay at the club was marred by injury but he was one of the great characters of soccer in the 1960s and is remembered for two brilliant goals for Villa against Spurs — the club's first win over the Londoners for years. Eventually he was left out of the League Cup Final against Birmingham City and was on the move again in the 1963 close season, joining Peterborough for £21,000. Villa was one of only half a dozen clubs 'The Doog' played for — but they still talk about him at Villa Park.

GERRY HITCHENS was a fine centre-forward who scored many goals for Aston Villa after he joined them from Cardiff City in 1957-8. Hichens was, in fact, a Midlander who was born in the Cannock Chase area and who lived most of his early life in Kidderminster where he made a name for himself in the Southern League. He was in the army when Villa signed him and it was not until 1959-60 that he was able to play as a full-time professional. Villa paid Cardiff £22,500 and Hitchens repaid them with some great goals, including five in an 11-1 win over Charlton Athletic. Season 1960-1 was his best when he missed only one League game and scored forty-one goals in all games. Only Chelsea's Jimmy Greaves bettered that in the First Division. It was this sort of form which made Inter Milan pay Villa £85,000 for Hitchens and the club were powerless to compete with the sort of wages that the Italians could offer. Hitchens won seven England caps, three of them with Villa in 1961.